THE APRON BOOK

❀

Making, Wearing, and Sharing
a Bit of Cloth and Comfort

EllynAnne Geisel

A Lark Production

Andrews McMeel
Publishing, LLC
Kansas City

To Hank, my prince charming

THE APRON BOOK

Copyright © 2006 by EllynAnne Geisel. All rights reserved. Printed in
China. No part of this book may be used or reproduced in any manner
whatsoever without written permission except in the case of reprints in the
context of reviews. For information, write Andrews McMeel Publishing,
LLC, an Andrews McMeel Universal company, 4520 Main Street,
Kansas City, Missouri 64111.

08 09 10 WKT 10 9 8 7

Library of Congress Cataloging-in-Publication Data

The apron book: making, wearing, and sharing a bit of cloth and
    comfort/[edited] by EllynAnne Geisel.
        p. cm.
    ISBN-13: 978-0-7407-6181-2
    ISBN-10: 0-7407-6181-1
     I. Geisel, EllynAnne.

    TT546.5.G45 2006
    391.4'4—dc22

                                                    2006042903

Book design by Diane Marsh

www.andrewsmcmeel.com

ATTENTION: SCHOOLS AND BUSINESSES

Andrews McMeel books are available at quantity discounts with bulk pur-
chase for educational, business, or sales promotional use. For information,
please write to: Special Sales Department, Andrews McMeel Publishing,
LLC, 4520 Main Street, Kansas City, Missouri 64111.

CONTENTS

FOREWORD

❧

AN APRON. Think fast! What comes to mind? Kitchens from the 1950s? June Cleaver? Gone and forgotten?

Well, not so fast! That's just what I thought until I met EllynAnne Geisel, a collector and cataloger of these housewife cover-ups. As EllynAnne unwrapped her treasures, my mind flashed back to my grandmother. There was Grandma in her tiny kitchen wiping her hands on her well-worn apron, which doubled as a pot holder when it was time to take out the roast. Then I pictured the organdy fantasy my mom wore for home dinner parties. And finally I remembered the gingham apron that was my first (and only) sewing badge project as a Brownie. Wish I had had the foresight to save a few of the full-length pinafore styles that were wedding shower presents. We can be careless with the fabric of our past.

But even without our own apron archives, thanks to EllynAnne we can travel back in time and revisit our past through the pages of this wonderful book. Who knew that vintage aprons would become a popular collectible or that so many stories could be told through artistic photographs of women wearing a simple piece of beloved cloth?

What is the allure of aprons? They tell the stories of our domestic lives. Wander through these pages as I have done. You may get misty-eyed as you read these women's words. Or you may be inspired to sew your own version with the simple directions provided. Or you just might be inspired to start your own collection. And you may find yourself tied to EllynAnne's apron strings . . . in the most positive way imaginable. Enjoy!

Ellen Levine
Editor-in-Chief, *Good Housekeeping*

A Loverly Apron

By Phyllis Reedy Young

Once upon a time

An apron or two

Hung out on the line

Twirling in the breeze

Under a sunny sky,

Flapping dry.

INTRODUCTION

HARRIET NELSON was my idol when I was growing up. She was everything I wanted to become—a wife, a mother, and a homemaker. I watched *The Adventures of Ozzie and Harriet* every week on television, reverently noting Harriet's clever way with her husband and sons, her calm demeanor, how she dressed up each day to stay at home taking care of her family. I loved how they worshipped her. And I *coveted* her apron.

My own mother was an amazing woman; long before it was the norm, she had a college degree, worked full time, and raised six children. She enjoyed her career and was successful at it, but as far as I was concerned, the job I wanted was Harriet's.

In 1966, I entered the University of Southern Hospitality with the goal of acquiring my Mrs. Degree. I got a tad sidetracked by bell-bottoms and rock-and-roll in the '60s, but deep down I remained committed to finding my Ozzie and becoming a full-time home-maker and mother. Married in 1975 and soon after the mother of two boys, I was blissfully living my girlhood dream.

For twenty-four years, I happily performed the domestic routines of old-fashioned housewifery. In 1999, when I sent my youngest son off to college, I turned my attention to the freelance writing career I had in mind for my empty-nest self. My first article was to be about a long-forgotten bit of vintage clothing—the apron.

I visited several thrift stores and picked up an assortment of stained, tattered aprons, some of them still quite beautiful, many of them examples of masterful sewing or embroidery. By the time I'd gathered a laundry basket full of aprons, I knew I was holding something extraordinary—a basket full of stories. From the intricately embroidered pink organza waist apron from the 1920s to the full body flour-sack apron from the 1940s to the "Sloppy Joe" barbecue apron from the 1950s, every apron spoke worlds of the heart and character of the people who had sewn and worn them.

Oh, I fell hard. Every apron I discovered I loved like a child, and every one of them wanted to tell me its story. And I was all ears! I wanted to know everything about the aprons I was collecting. I tended them, I studied them, I took them with me hither and yon and showed them off to everyone and anyone. And what I learned is that everybody has an apron story to share. So I gathered their stories and showcased their aprons in a traveling museum exhibit called *Apron Chronicles*. And then I started designing and making aprons myself. Suddenly, I was an artist with an amazing palette—the combinations of styles, fabrics, and adornments were infinite. My company, Apron Memories, is an outlet for all this creativity, and even though now I've become a "working woman" like my own mother, I still get to have that apron.

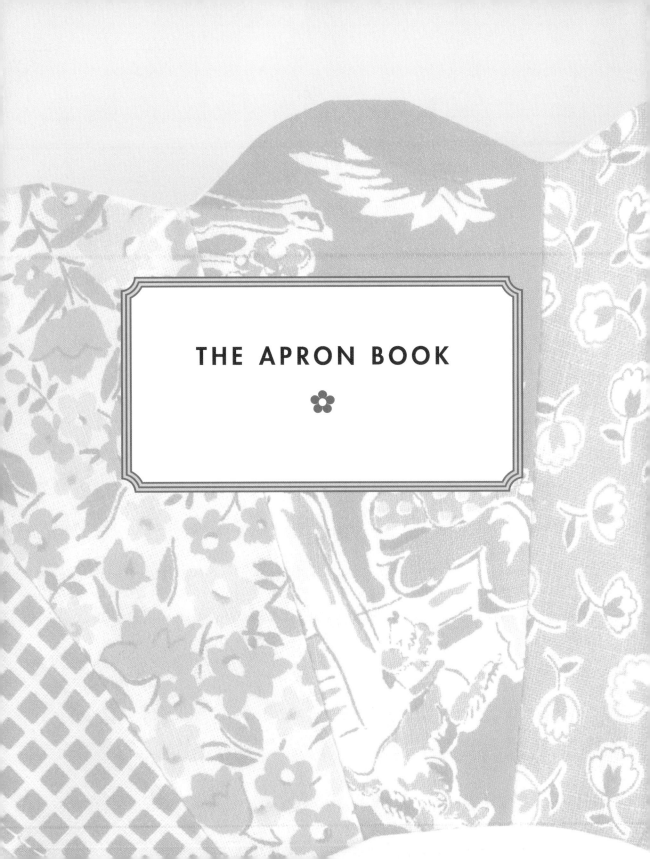

THE APRON BOOK

❀

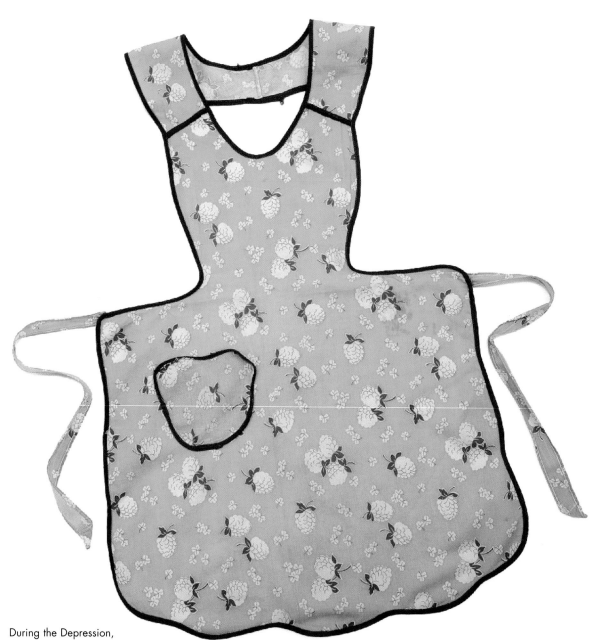

During the Depression,
homemakers unraveled the string
stitching of feed and flour sacks and converted the bags to "free
yardage," which they used to make clothing, quilts, and other
household items, like this slim-fitted feedsack apron.

chapter 1

APRONS: AN ODYSSEY

HOW DID aprons go from being an indispensable part of a woman's workaday wardrobe to an American icon to a sweet scrap of collectible nostalgia to one of the hottest sew-crafting trends going? The short answer is that unlike other clothing trends, the apron has always had a basic job to do. No amount of progress or technological advancement or fickle fashion tastes can change the fact that an apron has always been the best, most commonsensical means of covering up and protecting our clothes from grime.

The first reference to the apron is found in the Bible, no less. As the story goes, after Adam and Eve ate the fruit of the forbidden tree in the Garden of Eden, "Then the eyes of both were opened, and they knew that they were naked; and they sewed fig leaves together and made themselves aprons." (Genesis 3:7) Yikes. That would be an emergency apron! Well, there are plenty of people who feel naked without an apron on, and I'm one of them.

Fast forward several millennia to the wave of settlers and then immigrants who brought their sturdy aprons to America; they were simply styled, usually ankle-length, and made of rugged cloth. With clothing limited to a few pieces and washing such an arduous task, the long apron protected the dress underneath, allowing a dress to be worn several times before needing to be laundered. Flipping the apron from the soiled side to the clean was a good trick to extend the wear of the apron, too.

Worn by pioneers on the westward trail, these aprons were front and center for all the high drama and hard work it took to invent this country. Homesteading alongside the men, women tucked their dresses into apron waistbands to clear and plow the fields, then unfurled the aprons to carry grain to the chickens, gather eggs, and harvest vegetables from the garden. The apron was wrapped around the hands to remove a pan of hot biscuits from

the oven, it shooed flies from the table, and waved from the porch to signal that dinner was ready. On a single day, an apron might wipe a child's tears, the sweat off a brow, and flour from the hands, plus ward off a chill and hide a rifle. Now that's multitasking!

There wasn't anything a determined pioneer woman couldn't do when she donned her apron armor.

For those who stayed in cities and towns in the East and didn't board a Calistoga wagon, the all-purpose apron was the uniform of a domestic, a nurse, a seamstress, or a factory worker. And for those born with silver spoons in their mouths or well-heeled by marriage, aprons were a stylish accessory. With hired help tending to the more laborious homekeeping tasks, ladies of leisure engaged in stitchery. The apron became a canvas for the domestic art of embroidery. Tiny, immaculate stitches, delicate crochet, and other skilled needlecrafts turned the apron into art and a testament to refined feminine skills.

Fine cotton was hard to come by in the lean Depression years, but aprons continued to display creative handiwork on whatever cloth was available—a feed sack, carpenter's

This 1945 National Cotton Council publication touted many clever, thrifty ways to utilize feed-sack fabric in support of the "nation's effort to conserve and salvage for victory. A yard saved is a yard gained, for victory!"

cotton, or other recycled fabric. Gay embroidery and lighthearted motifs might brighten a threadbare wash-day apron, or a snip of rickrack the pocket of a kitchen apron—all good preparation to "make do without" later in support of the war effort of the 1940s.

The postwar era, though, was a time of exuberance and abundance, and the apron met its fun-filled future in the home of the middle class. En masse, homemakers sewed their own fashionable aprons from Simplicity or McCall's patterns, or from patterns offered by the newspaper syndicates. These designs reflected their aspirations to be modern, social, and stylish. Fabrics were bold with color, and adornments became more playful and less functional. At the same time, modern household appliances of the 1950s gave homemakers something previously unheard of—free time. Women spent this commodity with enthusiasm and sewed for their homes and themselves as never before, with their aprons the zenith of creative expression.

Good old-fashioned domestic humor, played out on the aprons of Americans everywhere. This one, perhaps, is a friendly warning shot across the bow of the war between the sexes that was just around the corner.

By now, homemakers were dressing up to stay home and had aprons for every chore and special occasion. They whipped up theme aprons, holiday aprons, aprons that matched the tablecloth on the bridge table, mother-daughter aprons, and daughter-dolly aprons. Aprons even became a venue for household humor, as a wearable billboard of bon mots. And for the first time, husbands donned aprons specific to their new pastime—manning the backyard barbecue. This was the official heyday of the American apron, with the kitchen drawer bursting with colorful expression.

Bennie Swanson

Mom was a smart, resourceful woman who handled difficulties with style and grace. She raised four daughters on her own, working long days scrubbing the cases and floors at a bakery and still managing to keep our home and sew all our clothes. During a visit with her when she was ill with Parkinson's later in her life, I discovered that she had saved the apron I made in my seventh grade home ec class. As I pulled it out of the drawer, I was thrust back to 1959. I could remember shopping with Mom for the fabric, my excitement at finally learning how to sew, and how proud I felt when she'd wear it to fix dinner. My memories of her are all tied up in the pretty strings of this apron—her strength and warmth and humor and the way she made me feel so special.

How could we celebrate the domestic life so dearly one day, wearing our cheerful aprons, and the next throw them down in a huff and become "liberated"? The Women's Movement of the 1960s saw a generation of women join the workforce to seek reward and fulfillment outside the home. Freed from their aprons' now strangulating strings, women tossed them—even those lovingly sewn by their own mothers and grandmothers—straight into the giveaway bag. And in that gesture, the historical connection that tied the modern woman to preceding generations of women was snipped. And so for a new generation of women whose association with the apron would be limited to a junior high sewing project, the apron was a relic of values and a lifestyle that no longer applied.

The good news is that the apron's disappearance of thirty years or so was just temporary.

Even though American women are now fully entrenched in the workplace, they are also back to cooking and sewing and crafting and nesting like never before. Seems like there are whole cable channels devoted to what amounts to the very fine art of home-making! So aprons are coming out of the attic and back to the kitchen. And if we aren't lucky enough to uncover a handed-down family apron, we're scouring thrift stores for them or sewing them up for ourselves. It's not just some retro trend or nostalgia for a simpler time that makes us want to take up our aprons again. It's part of a movement to reconnect to our love of home and family, as ever expressed in the many shapes and colors and adornments of the humble but lovely American apron.

chapter 2

THE ANATOMY OF AN APRON

AN APRON is like a woman—the bib is the bosom, the skirt is the lap, the pocket is the purse. And like an apron's human counterpart, it is the variations on these parts that make each one unique.

There have always been three basic types of aprons: workday, everyday, and fancy. Which apron you wore depended on what you were up to—a day of heavy cleaning, baking, or canning, gardening or sewing, making a quick dinner, or serving hors d'oeuvres at a cocktail party, for example. Workday aprons were the most protective; they're full-bodied with generous bib fronts and made of sturdy material. Everyday aprons were waist aprons or full styles, made of lighter material than workday aprons. And fancy aprons were rarely meant to be truly protective; they were mostly worn as accessories to an outfit or for special occasions, and were dainty confections made of delicate fabrics.

The basic apron constructions consist of the waist apron, the bib apron, and the smock apron. Any of these styles could serve as workday, everyday, or fancy aprons, depending on the fabric and decorative elements used. No matter what the style, the pocket was almost always a distinguishing feature. The pocket is my favorite part of vintage aprons because you learn so much about the person who wore them by looking at (or in) the pocket. You can tell whether the wearer was right- or left-handed by the pulled corners of the pocket, and an archaeological dig into an old apron pocket yields countless hankies and grocery lists.

We'll start sewing a basic apron wardrobe with the basic waist apron with basic pocket variations, designing and adding personal touches from there.

No matter what style of apron you're making, you're going to need the following basic materials:

- Fabric
- Thread
- Scissors
- Tape measure
- Pencil or chalk
- Pins
- Trim
- Hand sewing needle
- Sewing machine
- Iron

SELECTING FABRIC

CHOOSING YOUR fabric is the fun part of making an apron—you can mix and match among a myriad of options and never make the same apron twice. When selecting fabric, though, a tad of caution is called for. Keep these caveats in mind:

1. While your apron can be composed of an infinite combination of fabrics, it's good to work with materials that have compatible contents (cotton vs. synthetic, for example), weights (light cotton broadcloth vs. a heavy velvet), and care requirements (washer/dryer/iron temperature).

2. If you want to work with vintage fabric, hold your yardage in the light and examine it for weaknesses, tears, or small holes. Washing puts stress on any fabric, and you don't want to use fabric that won't be able to weather regular laundering.

3. Prewash your fabric and dry it on medium heat for maximum shrinkage. Then iron the fabric before laying out and cutting your pattern pieces.

As with any sewing project, using plaids, checks, or stripes depends entirely on your sewing skills. All of these designs require precise matching when laying out your pattern, cutting, and sewing. If a full-scale painstakingly constructed all-plaid apron is beyond your abilities (or patience!), consider mixing your favorite plaid with a solid or with a totally contrasting fabric.

Look for ways to incorporate vintage fabrics or to recycle favorite fabrics from other sources. Dish towels, sheets and pillowcases, curtains, tablecloths, napkins—any of these alone or mixed with contemporary fabrics can make for fun combinations. Use a bit of vintage fabric to accent a pocket or border a hem on your modern creation. Or use snips of vintage or contrasting fabric to make the panel apron (two of my favorites are below), a combination of meticulous engineering and skillful sewing. On the other hand, I'll take the crooked seams and mismatched everything of a well-loved apron any day!

Things to Know Before You Sew

The following is a crib sheet for sewing terms and tips, and a guide to the visual aids you'll see sprinkled throughout the patterns and sewing instructions for our aprons.

The **RIGHT SIDE** of the fabric is the side that has the sharpest, clearest design. The **WRONG SIDE** is the flip side, or back side, of the right side of the fabric.

RIGHT SIDE UP means you should place the fabric so the design is facing you.

WRONG SIDE UP means you should place the fabric so the back side of the fabric is facing you.

Press with a warm iron when you see this: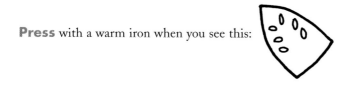

A **RAW EDGE** is an unfinished/unsewn edge.

A **REGULAR STITCH** is a stitch length of 2.5, or 10 to 12 stitches per inch. On the stitch-length dial on your sewing machine, set it to between 2 and 3.

A **TOPSTITCH** is a regular stitch that is sewn on the right side of the fabric.

A **BASTING STITCH** is the widest stitch you can set on your sewing machine. This is a loose stitch that allows you to arrange material in place before permanent stitching. Turn the stitch length dial to the highest setting for a basting stitch.

BACKSTITCH at the end of each sewing step to prevent unraveling. When you reach the end of a row of sewing, set to reverse, sew slowly backward for 1/2 inch, then sew forward to the end.

Good to Know

Using the tips and tricks below will help you construct a neat, crisp apron in the end and avoid the frustrations created by taking shortcuts!

- Before cutting, wash and dry material as you intend to launder the finished garment.
- Measure and mark your patterns on sturdy muslin, butcher paper, or a stiff liner, then cut out the individual pieces to lay out as a pattern on your real apron fabric.
- If you're new to sewing, cut out a pattern on inexpensive muslin and sew a practice apron before cutting your real fabric.
- Measure a seam and press it before sewing; then press once again after sewing.
- Clean your cutting surface thoroughly before laying out your fabric.
- If you don't have a large enough table to lay out your fabric and cut your pattern, clear and clean a place on the floor.
- Use two well-sharpened pairs of scissors: one just for cutting fabric, the other for cutting everything else.
- Test your stitching on a sample swatch of fabric to determine whether your stitches are too tight or too loose.

Even Cinderella gets her own basic waist apron, courtesy of a Disney promotion, circa late 1940s.

every apron tells a story

Eleanor Rusler

My Grandma Angelina was a whiz at sewing; everyone said her hands were blessed. She could copy anything at all, so she made clothes for our family and for others, to supplement the family income. She'd put newspapers on the floor and make her own apron and dress patterns. She had a portable Singer sewing machine, which she put on the kitchen table.

I've always loved to bake and when Grandma would come to our house to visit, she'd sit at one end of the kitchen table sewing and I'd be at the other end, making a pie. I remember once I was rolling a crust and when I picked it up it fell apart. "That's okay, baby," Grandma told me, and somehow she put that crust back together. This apron, which she made from her own newspaper pattern, reminds me of that day because she was wearing it when she rescued that crust. Grandma could fix anything.

Basic Waist Apron

YOU WILL NEED: 1 yard (36 inches) of fabric, 42–45 inches wide; matching thread, scissors, a ruler, a pencil, and straight pins.

CUTTING THE PATTERN

Step 1: Place your fabric so the right side is facing up and the longest edge of fabric is horizontal.

Step 2: Measure and mark with your pencil a line 20 inches above the bottom edge of the fabric and cut out this piece. This is your apron's skirt.

Step 3: Cut out these pieces as illustrated in Figure 1.1:

- Two 4 x 30-inch ties
- One 5 x 19-inch waistband
- Two 8 x 8-inch pockets

Figure 1.1

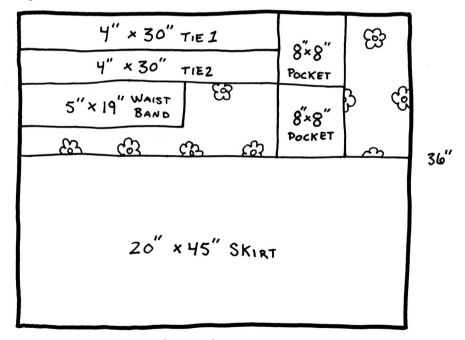

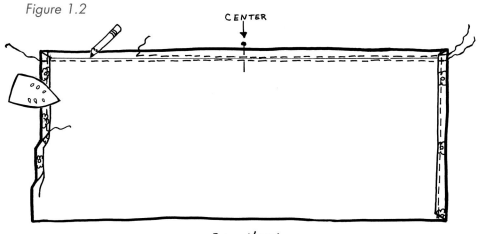

Figure 1.2

CENTER

BACK VIEW

SEWING THE APRON

For the skirt: Hemming the side edges

Step 1: Lay your fabric wrong side up. (See Figure 1.2.) Turn in the left raw edge $1/4$ inch and do the same with the right raw edge. Press with a warm iron. Fold both edges in $1/4$ inch once more and press.

Step 2: Stitch a narrow hem down each edge.

Preparing the gathers

Step 1: At the top raw edge, find the center of your apron's skirt and mark it with a straight pin. (See Figure 1.2.)

Step 2: Measure $5/8$ inch down. Mark this measurement from one side of the apron to the other.

Step 3: Set the machine for a loose basting stitch (4–5). Pull the thread from the needle and bobbin so you have approximately 6 inches of excess before you start sewing.

Step 4: Sew across the top of the skirt $5/8$ inch from the raw edge. Before clipping the threads, pull 6 inches from the needle and bobbin as above. Now sew a second basting stitch just above the first, $1/2$ inch from the raw edge, again pulling the threads 6 inches from each end before clipping.

Step 5: Reset your machine to a regular stitch (2–3).

Figure 1.3

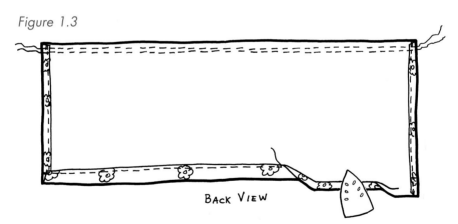

BACK VIEW

Hemming the bottom edge

Step 1: Turn the bottom raw edge up $1/4$ inch and press. (See Figure 1.3.) Fold the bottom up $1 3/4$ inches and press again.

Step 2: Stitch a narrow hem edge to edge. *Note that the top edge remains raw.* Set the skirt aside.

Figure 1.4   BACK VIEW

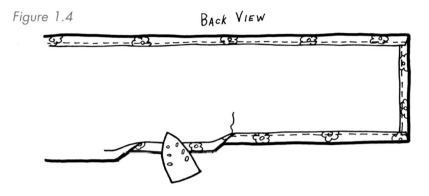

For the ties

Step 1: Lay one tie wrong side up. Turn in the right raw edge ¼ inch and
         press. Fold in ¼ inch once more and press.

Step 2: Stitch from end to end.

Step 3: Repeat the steps above for the second tie.

Step 4: Turn in the top and bottom raw edges ¼ inch and press. (See Figure
         1.4.) Fold in ¼ inch once more and press.

Step 5: Stitch from end to end. *Note that the left edge remains raw.*
         Set the ties aside.

> ### TIE VARIATION
> To create pointed tie ends,
> fold down the right side of the finished
> end 45 degrees and press.
> (See Figure 1.5.)

Figure 1.5   BACK VIEW

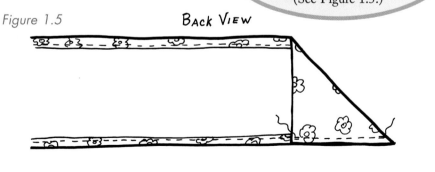

For the waistband

Step 1: With wrong side up, turn the left and right raw edges ¹/2 inch and press. (See Figure 1.6.)

Step 2: Turn up the bottom raw edge ¹/2 inch and press. *Note the top edge remains raw.* Set the waistband aside.

Figure 1.6

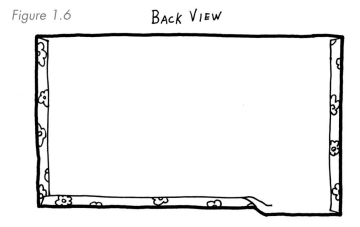

BACK VIEW

For a basic pocket

Step 1: Pin together the two 8-inch squares so the right sides are facing each other. (See Figure 1.7.) Starting on the bottom, stitch around the entire square ¹/2 inch from the edge, leaving a ¹/2-inch opening at the bottom in order to turn the pocket.

Step 2: Trim the corners as shown.

Step 3: Turn the pocket right side out, pushing it through the opening. Turn the raw edges back into the opening and press the entire pocket.

TIP: A crochet hook or the eraser end of a pencil are good turner-helpers.

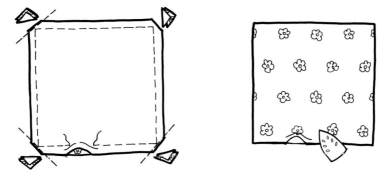

Figure 1.7

Figure 1.8

FRONT VIEW

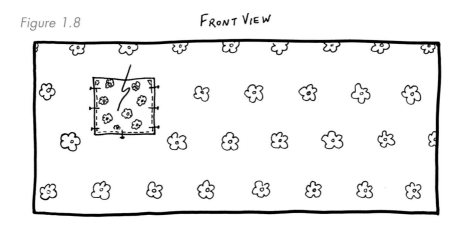

Step 4: Measure 4 inches down from the skirt's top edge and 7 inches in from the right or left side. (See Figure 1.8.) Pin your pocket here.

Step 5: Topstitch around the two sides and the bottom of the pocket. Backstitch at the beginning and end points for added strength.

TIP: It's much easier to apply pockets or other embellishments to the apron skirt before gathering the skirt. So plan and execute your decorations *before* you gather the skirt and complete the apron.

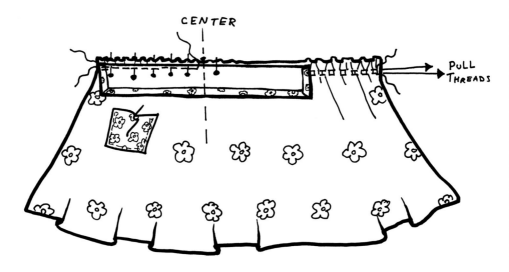

CENTER

PULL
THREADS

Figure 1.9

Gathering the skirt

Step 1: Place the right side of the waistband on the right side of the skirt. (See Figure 1.9.) The raw edges should meet at the top.

Step 2: Mark the center of your waistband with a straight pin and match it up to the pin at the center of your apron's skirt. Pin the centers together at this point.

Step 3: Gently pull both threads from the right side of the skirt, adjusting the gathers that form so they run evenly along the waistband, pinning as you go along.

Step 4: When you're happy with the gathers, sew the waistband to the apron's skirt 1/2 inch from the top edge.

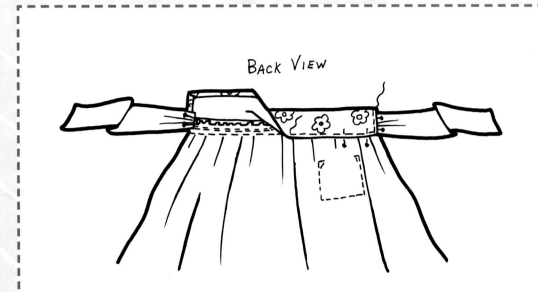

BACK VIEW

Figure 1.10

Finishing the waistband and ties

Step 1: Set your machine to a loose basting stitch (4–5).

Step 2: Fold the waistband over the back side of the apron's skirt. (See Figure 1.10.)

Step 3: Pin the waistband to the back side of the skirt and baste stitch from end to end.

Step 4: Slide the unfinished ends of the ties into the waistband openings and pin.

Step 5: Reset your machine to a regular stitch (2–3).

Step 6: Stitch close to the edge all along the sides and bottom of the waistband. Remove the basting stitches.

Figure 1.11

Voilà! A finished waist apron. Read on to find out how to make yours unique or make a gift extraspecial for someone.

This coordinating bit of a vintage rosy hankie is the decorative focal point of the pocket design.

A Pocketful of Miracles

ockets are where you can really start to express yourself on your aprons. You can use the same fabric as the rest of your apron and play with the shape of or the decoration on the pocket. You can also use a contrasting fabric for the whole pocket or just the inside lining of the pocket. Or you can use a quilt square, pot holder, or vintage hankie for your pocket material. Here are some variations on the basic pocket:

Figure 2.1

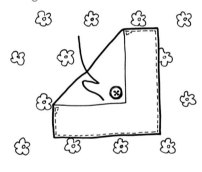

Flap pocket

Fold down one corner of sewn, turned, and pressed pocket to make a flap. Anchor the flap with an old button. Measure and attach to the apron as with a basic pocket. (See Figure 2.1.)

Figure 2.2

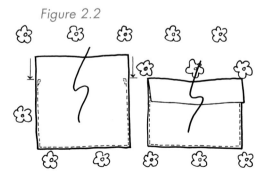

Foldover pocket

Measure and attach to the apron as with a basic pocket, but begin stitching 2 inches down from the top edge. Then fold the top edge down. (See Figure 2.2.)

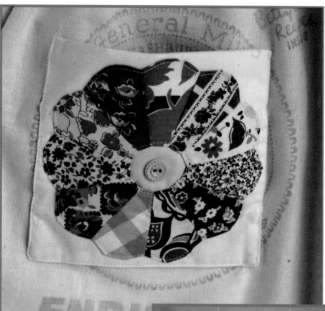

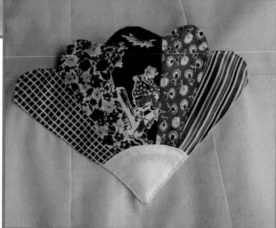

These pockets are themselves patchwork works of art. The flower is assembled and sewn together first, then attached to a basic square pocket, while the scallop is stitched together quilt-style, then attached directly to the apron.

Pocket pizzazz

For slightly more adventurous pockets, think of shapes and colors as your palette. For instance, cut a shape from a contrasting fabric (a tulip shape or a heart, for example), finish the edges, and attach to the skirt per basic pocket directions, page 22.

This heart-shaped pocket is a simple, romantic touch.

Contrasting fabrics and a shaped pocket give this vintage bib apron distinction.

ALL THAT JAZZ

THERE ARE countless easy ways to jazz up your aprons. Match the pocket, ties, and waistband fabric, then use a coordinating or contrasting fabric for your apron's skirt. Or sew a big button on the waistband of your apron, then sew a loop to the corner of a dish towel and hang the towel from the button. Or hang a hot pad from the button. Handy! Personalize your apron with rickrack, bias tape or ribbon edging, or lace flourishes. Or tuck a pretty hankie in your pocket. If you're having a luncheon or a tea or a wedding shower and you really want to act snazzy, sew napkins to match your apron (14-inch squares topstitched on all sides).

Creative use of appliqué and embroidery disguise the hidden pockets behind the Southern belle's skirt.

Basic Bib Apron

This crocheted vintage flower pot holder
brings the basic sewn pocket to life.

YOU WILL NEED: 1⅛ yards of fabric, 44–55 inches wide; 9 yards of seam
binding, matching thread, scissors, a ruler, a pencil, and straight pins.

CUTTING THE PATTERN

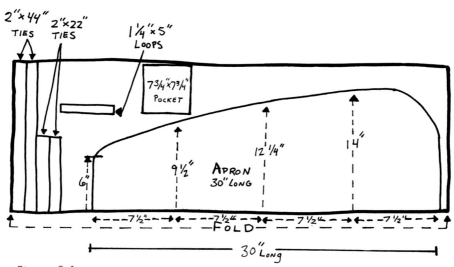

Figure 3.1

Step 1: Place your fabric so the wrong side is facing up and the longest edge of fabric is horizontal.

Step 2: Fold the fabric in half. Now the right side is facing up.

Step 3: Measure the illustrated pattern pieces and cut them out:
- One apron bib body
- Two 1¼ x 5-inch strips (these are your loops)
- Two strips 2 x 44 inches and two strips 2 x 22 inches (these are your ties)
- Two 7¾-inch squares for the pocket

SEWING THE APRON

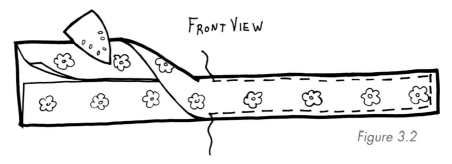

Figure 3.2

For the loops

Step 1: Turn in the long (5-inch) edges ¼ inch and press.

Step 2: Fold the loop in half lengthwise with the wrong sides together and press.

Step 3: Topstitch along all four sides, staying close to the edge. (See Figure 3.2.)

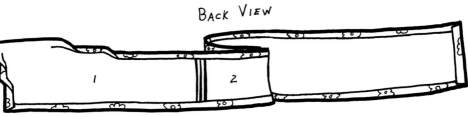

Figure 3.3

For the ties

Step 1: With the right sides together pin one long 2 x 44-inch strip to a shorter 2 x 22-inch strip at the 2-inch end, then sew a ½-inch seam. Open the seam and press it flat. (See Figure 3.3.)

Step 2: Repeat with the other 2 x 44-inch and 2 x 22-inch strips.

Step 3: Turn in the long top raw edge and the bottom raw edge ¼ inch and press. Turn the edges in ¼ inch once more and press.

Step 4: Repeat as above on both short side edges.

Step 5: Topstitch a narrow hem around the four folded and pressed edges.

FRONT VIEW

— 4" — | — 4" —

12"

Figure 3.4

To attach the ties and loops to the apron

Step 1: Fold the apron in half vertically and mark the center with a pin. (See Figure 3.4.) Unfold and lay right side up.

Step 2: From the marked center, measure 4 inches to the right and left and mark these spots. Pin the ties at these spots.

Step 3: From the outer edges of the ties, measure 12 inches along the apron edge and mark these spots. Pin the loops at these spots.

To edge the apron

Step 1: Match the raw edges of the wrong side of the apron fabric with the right side of the bias tape and pin in place. (See Figure 3.5.)

Step 2: Sew all around the apron edges.

Step 3: Turn the tape up and over to the other side of the apron and pin in place. (See Figure 3.6.)

Step 4: Topstitch all around the bias tape, close to the edge.

Step 5: Flip the loops and ties over the stitched bias tape. Sew the loops and ties to the bias tape. Sew twice to reinforce these stress points.

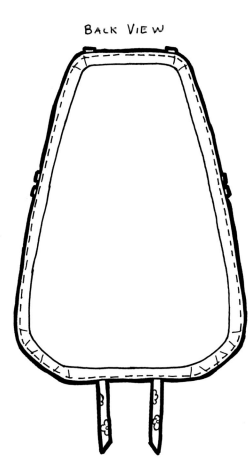

BACK VIEW

Figure 3.5

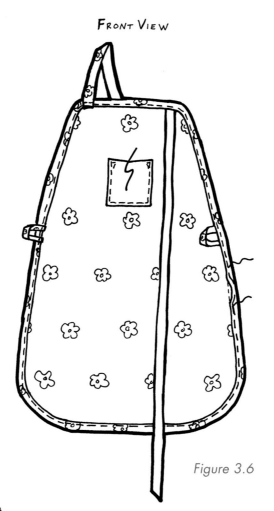

FRONT VIEW

Figure 3.6

For the pocket

Step 1: Pin together the two pocket squares so the right sides are facing each other. Starting at the bottom, stitch around the entire square $1/2$ inch from the edge, leaving a $1/2$-inch opening at the bottom in order to turn the pocket.

Step 2: Trim the corners as shown in Figure 3.7.

Step 3: Turn the pocket right side out, pushing it through the opening. Turn the raw edges back into the opening and press the entire pocket.

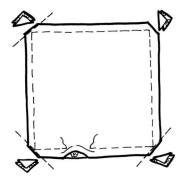

Figure 3.7

Step 4: Measure 5 inches from the top center of the apron and mark. Pin your pocket here.

Step 5: Topstitch around the two sides and the bottom of the pocket. Backstitch at the beginning and end points for reinforcement.

TIP:
For perfect pocket placement, fold the apron front in half, wrong sides together, and lightly crease. Fold the pocket in half, wrong sides together, and lightly crease. Unfold both and at your mark, match the creases and pin in place 5 inches from the top.

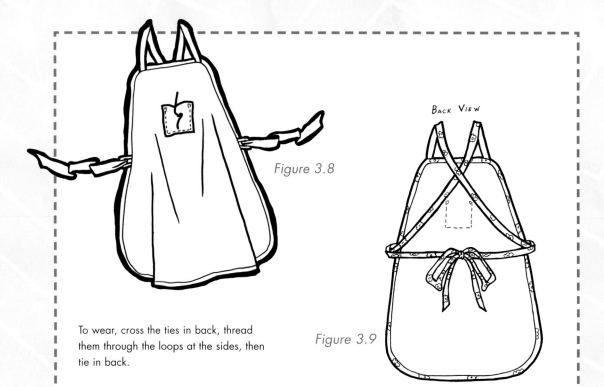

Figure 3.8

To wear, cross the ties in back, thread them through the loops at the sides, then tie in back.

Back View

Figure 3.9

MORE OF THAT JAZZ

MAKE THE ties using two different fabrics. Cut two sets of material for the ties, each from different fabrics. Pin the contrasting pieces, right sides together, and sew a narrow seam around three edges, leaving one end open. Turn the tie right side out through the open end, then finish the remaining raw edge by turning in and sewing closed.

Also, instead of a basic sewn pocket, add other adornments, such as an appliqué or a handful of pretty flat buttons arranged in the shape of a flower. And if you have the ability, there's no better canvas for embroidered embellishments than the front of a basic bib apron. Go to town!

Basic Smock Apron

2½ yards of fabric, 42–45 inches wide;
matching thread, scissors, a ruler, a pencil, and straight pins.

CUTTING THE PATTERN

NOTE: The front and back of the basic smock apron are identical, so the pattern pieces must be laid out in the same direction.

Step 1: Place your fabric so the wrong side is facing up and the longest edge is horizontal.

Step 2: Fold the bottom half of the fabric up and match the edges at the top. Now the right side is facing up.

Step 3: From the left, fold the fabric in half over to the right, matching the edges.

Step 4: Measure 7 inches in from the left side and draw a line from top to bottom. Cut along the measured line and set this fabric aside. This portion is for the pocket and waistband.

Step 5: Cut out these pieces as illustrated in Figure 4.1:

- Two apron bodies
- Four 2½ x 9-inch shoulder ties
- Four 2½ x 30-inch waist ties

Figure 4.1

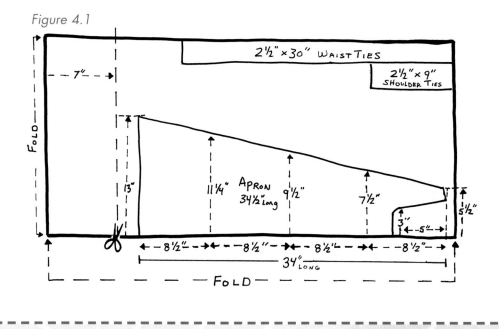

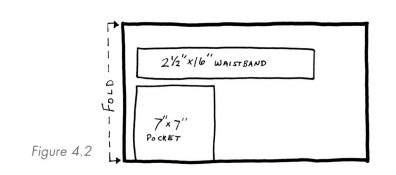

Figure 4.2

Step 6: With the fabric you set aside, fold and cut out these pieces as illustrated in Figure 4.2:
- Two 7 x 7-inch pockets
- Two 2^{1}/$_{2}$ x 16-inch waistbands

SEWING THE APRON

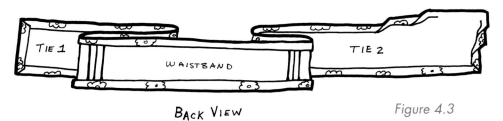

BACK VIEW

Figure 4.3

For the waistband and waist ties

Step 1: With the right sides together, pin one waist tie to the waistband at a 2^{1}/$_{2}$-inch edge and sew a ^{1}/$_{2}$-inch seam. Pin a second waist tie to the waistband's remaining raw 2^{1}/$_{2}$-inch edge and sew a ^{1}/$_{2}$-inch seam.

Step 2: Turn the entire length of the top and bottom raw edges of waistband/ties ^{1}/$_{4}$ inch and press. (See Figure 4.3.) Turn the folded edges ^{1}/$_{4}$ inch once more and press.

Step 3: Turn and press the two short raw edges as above.

Step 4: Topstitch a narrow hem around the four folded and pressed edges.

Step 5: Repeat Steps 1–4 with the remaining waistband and ties. Set aside.

For the shoulder ties

Step 1: Fold in the long raw edges ¼ inch and press. Turn the folded edge ¼ inch once more and press.

Step 2: Turn and press the short raw edges as above.

Step 3: Topstitch a narrow hem around the four folded and pressed edges. Set aside.

Figure 4.4

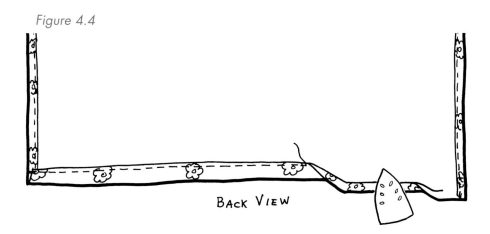

BACK VIEW

For the apron body

Step 1: Lay the fabric so that the wrong side is up. Turn the raw edges in ¼ inch and press (See Figure 4.4.) Turn the folded edges in ¼ inch once more and press.

Step 2: Stitch a narrow hem around the apron's folded and pressed edges.

VARIATION:
A coordinating seam binding can be sewn around the apron's edges.

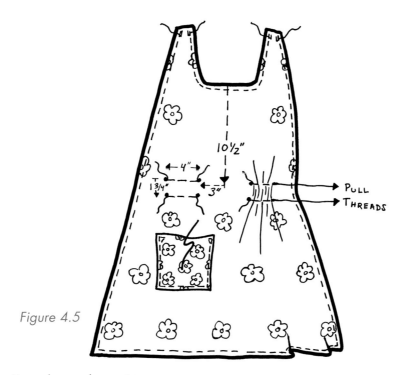

Figure 4.5

To gather at the waist

Step 1: Find the center point at the neckline and mark. (See Figure 4.5.)

Step 2: Measure 10½ inches down and mark.

Step 3: Measure over 3 inches on both sides and mark.

Step 4: From these marks, measure over an additional 4 inches on both sides and mark (remove the markers on the center line). These are the gathering areas for the top row of gathers.

Step 5: Measure 1¾ inches down from each of your four remaining marks and mark again. These are the gathering areas for the bottom row of gathers.

Step 6: Set your machine to a loose basting stitch (4–5) and baste between the two marks on both sides for the top and bottom rows of gathers.

Step 7: Repeat Steps 1-6 for the back side of the apron body. Reset your machine to a regular stitch (2–3).

For the pocket

Step 1: Pin together the two pocket squares so the right sides are facing each other. (See Figure 4.6.) Starting at the bottom, stitch around the entire square $1/2$ inch from the edge, leaving a $1/2$-inch opening at the bottom in order to turn the pocket.

Step 2: Trim the corners as shown.

Step 3: Turn the pocket right side out, pushing it through the opening. Turn the raw edges back into the opening and press the entire pocket.

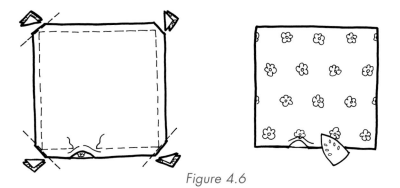

Figure 4.6

Step 4: On the right side of the front apron body, measure 4 inches down from the bottom row of basting stitches and $3^1/2$ inches from the left or right outside edge (your preference as to which side). Pin your pocket here.

Step 5: Topstitch around the two sides and the bottom of the pocket. Backstitch at the beginning and end points to reinforce them.

To complete the gathers

Step 1: Gently pull the basting threads on both sides of the apron to create even gathers. (See Figure 4.5.) Repeat with the bottom row of basting threads. Pin the gathers in place.

Step 2: Sew the gathers in place, backstitching at the beginning and end to reinforce them. Remove the pins.

Step 3: Repeat Steps 1–2 for the back apron body.

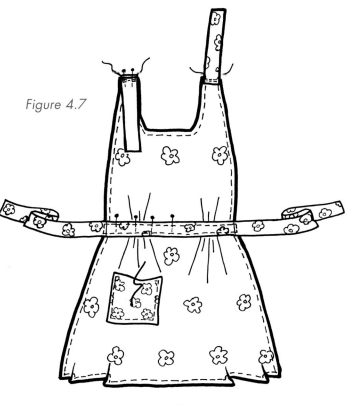

Figure 4.7

FRONT VIEW

To attach the shoulder ties

Step 1: Pin the ties at the shoulders with the right side of the ties facing the right side of the apron body. (See Figure 4.7.)

Step 2: Sew the straps to the shoulders with a 1/2-inch seam. Remove the pins and flip the ties up. Press them flat at the seams.

Step 3: Measure 1/4 inch up from the seams and topstitch across each tie. Add a second row of topstitching 1/4 inch above the first to reinforce them.

Step 4: Repeat Steps 1–3 to attach the ties to the back apron body.

To attach the waistband

Step 1: Find the center point of the waistband/ties and mark with a pin.

Step 2: Find the center point between the rows of gathering and mark with a pin.

Step 3: Match the pin points and the side edges, placing the wrong side of the waistband to the right side of the apron body and covering the gathering stitches. (See Figure 4.7.) Pin the waistband on all four sides to the apron body.

Step 4: Topstitch around all four sides close to the edge.

Step 5: Topstitch 1/4 inch in from the edge around all four sides to reinforce them.

Step 6: Repeat Steps 1–5 for the back apron body.

Figure 4.8

To assemble

Tie the shoulder ties into bows or knots. Slip the apron over your head and tie at the sides in looping bows or knots. Adjust the fit by fiddling with the shoulder ties. In the future, put on and remove over your head, so not to disturb your shoulder tie fit.

Dick Amman

My mom was a devoted wife and mother. The first up every morning, she would don her very practical apron, which was usually made out of floral feed-sack material and went over her head and buttoned or tied behind her back. She'd prepare lunches for my five sisters and me, and one for Dad, too, all packed in brown paper bags with our names on them.

Mother was thrifty; we were instructed to bring the bags home each day because she wanted to get at least two weeks' use from the bags before replacing them. One April Fool's Day, she deliberately switched "lunch orders" in newly issued bags so we'd be surprised by the contents of our sacks in front of our peers. Even our father wasn't spared; upon opening his lunch, he discovered a newspaper and one hard-boiled egg.

About three o'clock in the afternoon, Mom would straighten the house, vacuuming and dusting, and by the time we walked in from school, she'd be in the kitchen with her apron on, preparing the evening meal. Every dinner was complete with meat, potatoes, salad, two vegetables, and bread and butter. And the dining table was always set with a vase of fresh flowers or green cuttings.

When dinner was just about ready, she'd go freshen up, changing clothes and putting on makeup. When one of my sisters once asked her how come she "got ready" and changed clothes right before dinner, Mom smiled and said, "Because my husband is coming home." When our father walked into the house from work, he was greeted with a delicious home-cooked meal on the table and Mom, all decked out in a fresh, pretty apron.

chapter 3

APRONS IN THE KITCHEN

❁

WEARING AN apron is just good sense, especially in the kitchen. It's your armor against the splatter. It's your oven mitt, ingredient gatherer, jar opener, dishrag, counter wiper, window defogger, and smoke swatter at whatever moment you might need any one of these things. And when things go wrong—as they sometimes do—it'll dry your tears after a good cry. How do you get along in a kitchen without an apron? You don't.

This is why for centuries, a homemaker would put on her apron when she first stepped into the kitchen early in the morning and wouldn't take it off until the end of the day. There was simply too much to do and too many ways an apron could help you get the job done. A veritable wearable aide-de-camp—I like that.

Some of my favorite aprons are the well-worn workhorses of the kitchen. A threadbare smock apron that baked a thousand loaves of bread. The waist apron with a soft old dish towel attached by a big button. Even the modern bib-style chef's apron, with its air of crisp efficiency and authority.

Bib or smock aprons are especially smart kitchen wear for those big baking, cooking, and frying extravaganzas that seemed so doable when you volunteered to make your famous meatballs and spaghetti sauce for the neighborhood pre-Halloween party or to make five cheesecakes for a friend's daughter's baby shower. When you have that kind of work to do, the goal is maximum coverage. Your apron can be pretty, but it shouldn't be fussy, because it needs to be functional and protective above all else.

For everyday meal preparation or simple baking, I like an apron with a twist, like the half apron with built-in pot holders from my collection on the next page. The tulip hot pads aren't even a tad scorched or stained, a testament to the original owner's kitchen prowess. I wish I knew her secret! Knowing where my hot pads are when the timer dings makes this one of my favorite aprons. (Maybe that's what she thought, too.)

This tulip-shaped potholder is a quirky, sweet homemade touch. A pair of plain or decorative store-bought mitts will do just as well.

Waist Apron with Potholders

To add dangled hot pads to the basic waist apron (see instructions on page 17), you will need four hotpads and two strips of fabric. For the fabric length, measure from the raw edge at the skirt's waist to the bottom of the skirt's hem and add 1 inch; the width measurement of the fabric is the same as the hot pad plus 1 inch.

Hem the long sides and bottom edge of both pieces of fabric $1/2$ inch, as you did with the skirt of your apron. The finished width should be the same as the hot pad. Sew two pads together, stitching around three sides and leaving the top side open like a pocket. Pin the double pad to the fabric strip, matching the bottom and side edges, and topstitch. Repeat with the other pair of pads and fabric strip. Pin the strips to the gathered waist of the apron, with the wrong side of the dangled strips against the right side of the apron skirt. Match the side edges and top raw edges; pin, and sew as directed for basic waist apron.

every apron tells a story

Julia Child

My mother never cooked nor wore an apron. I didn't either until I met my husband.

Newly married in 1949, Paul and I moved to France, the result of his employment with the diplomatic service. He spoke beautiful French, and I spoke none. I managed for a time with a few phrases here and there, but I was motivated to learn the language following my introduction to French cuisine. Once I tasted French food, I knew I wanted to learn French cooking, and at the Cordon Bleu cooking school, all professional instruction was in French.

Since that time, I have always worn the chef-type blue denim apron with a towel stuck on the side under the string. It's a working apron, not a dainty thing. "Dainty" doesn't look professional in the kitchen. When Paul cooked with me, he wore the same type of apron, folding the bib at the waist and hanging a towel from the apron pocket.

I enjoy preparing meals that will be shared with others. I believe that families who eat together stay together, and Paul and I always had breakfast and most of our meals with each other. After retirement, we often ate at home in our kitchen. Upon his death in 1994, Paul and I had eaten together for almost fifty years.

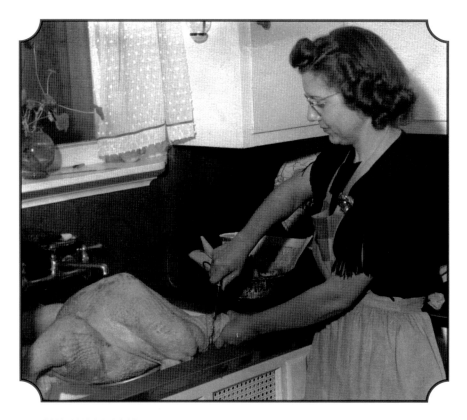

MY HUSBAND and I were married on September 20, 1942. We spent our first Thanksgiving with his family. Someone got the turkey from a local grocer instead of the butcher, and being a city lady, my mother-in-law had no idea how to remove the innards and finish plucking off the pinfeathers of a turkey that had not been properly "dressed." The farm girl from Kansas (that would be me) knew exactly what to do. Borrowing an apron to tie over my nice holiday dress, I carried the carcass to the sink and proceeded to get it ready for cooking. And to think my mother-in-law had someone else in mind for her son to marry— a city girl, of course!

—Vonetta Lee

POKE AN EGG with a small sewing needle before hard-boiling and the egg will peel like Gypsy Rose Lee.

> LIGHTEN PANCAKES BY substituting ricotta cheese for the recipe's milk.

Kids in the Kitchen

Most children can't wait to be old enough to help out in the kitchen. Who can blame them? Good smells, tasty snacks, licking beaters, and permission to make a mess with impunity! Those plastic "let's pretend" kitchens are fine for young child's play, but plastic for a four-year-old doesn't hold a candle to a real kitchen. And a real kid making real food in a real kitchen needs a real apron!

every apron tells a story
Betty Geer Johnson

Dorothy LeBaron Braun and I have been friends since we were three years old. We lived in the same neighborhood growing up, and our daddies worked together. I had three siblings and just loved to go to Dorothy's house, because she was an only child and received lots of doting attention. When I went over to her house, that attention was generously lavished on me, too.

Our favorite thing to do was bake cookies, and Dorothy's mother, a virtuoso homemaker, allowed us to do almost everything ourselves. Of course, if we needed her, she was right there to help. We just loved rolling the dough over and over with our little pins.

One year, our parents vacationed together in Mexico and brought back these souvenir aprons for Dorothy and me. The aprons were fancily embroidered and crocheted around the edges. They had pulled threadwork tied into the prettiest designs.

Dorothy grew up to become a home ec teacher, and I became a homemaker. We remain the best of friends.

Versatile and Delicious Sugar Cookies

3/4 cup butter, softened at room temperature

1 cup sugar

2 eggs

1/2 teaspoon almond flavoring

1 teaspoon baking powder

2 1/2 cups flour

1 teaspoon salt

Preheat the oven to 375 degrees. Cream the butter and sugar. Add the eggs and flavoring; beat until fluffy. Stir together the remaining dry ingredients and mix into the creamed mixture. Chill 2–3 hours. Roll out on a lightly floured surface to no more than 1/2 inch thick and cut into shapes using cookie cutters, a biscuit cutter, or the floured rim of a juice glass. Sprinkle the cookies with additional sugar. Place on ungreased cookie sheets in the preheated oven for 6–8 minutes or until delicately golden.

Makes about 4 dozen cookies.

PAINTBRUSH COOKIES: Blend 1 egg yolk with 1/4 teaspoon water. Divide the mixture into several cups and add a drop or more of different food colorings to each. Paint designs on the cookies before baking in the preheated oven.

As a little girl, Cristie
Coffman chose the yellow gingham and watched her
grandma Lila cut and sew this apron for her. The
flower pot–shaped pocket and rickrack flowers were
her grandma's whimsical idea.

ICE CUBES MADE from
the beverage you are drinking
won't dilute the drink.

Vintage children's aprons are probably the most valued as a collectible. Because children didn't have a wardrobe of aprons, the single apron they did have was worn hard, and once beyond repair, was recycled to the rag bag. Those who are lucky enough to still have their childhood apron speak lovingly of the woman who sewed it, the circumstances of its presentation, when it was worn, and how proud they felt wearing it when deemed old enough to help out in the kitchen. Aprons for children were diminutive versions of grown-up styles, with the addition of an exaggerated pouffy bow that was all little girl.

Even if you don't own a sewing machine, you can still make a darling child's apron out of a bandana or a cloth napkin or even a kitchen towel, just by using a threaded needle to attach ribbons to either side for waist ties. Otherwise, sew a simple child's apron following the directions on the next page, using fabric and materials you select together. This apron is easily enlivened, something you and your child can do together, making a memory in the process.

A Basic Child's Apron

YOU WILL NEED:

$1/2$ yard 36-inches-wide muslin, $1/4$ yard patterned fabric or scraps, 8 feet prefolded bias tape, matching thread, scissors, a ruler, a pencil, straight pins.

ADD A TEASPOON of lemon juice to the cooking water for whiter, fluffier rice.

NOTE: Muslin shrinks, so it must be washed and dried before cutting.

CUTTING THE PATTERN

Step 1: Place your muslin fabric so the longest edge is horizontal. Muslin has no right or wrong side. (See Figure 5.1.)

Step 2: Fold the material in half down the middle. Measure and cut a 14-inch square along the folded edge. The corners may be left square or rounded. This is the apron skirt.

Step 3: Cut a piece of fabric 2¼ x 30 inches. This is the sash casing.

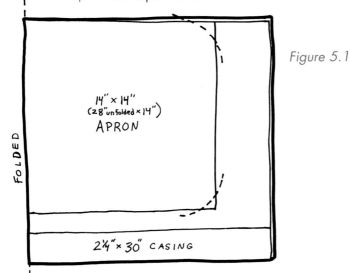

Figure 5.1

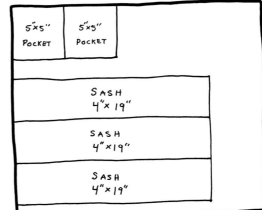

Figure 5.2

Step 4: Place your patterned fabric right side up. Cut out these pieces as illustrated in Figure 5.2:
- Three 4 x 19-inch strips (sash)
- Two 5 x 5-inch pockets

SEWING THE APRON

For the sash

Step 1: With right sides together, pin sash strip 1 and strip 2 at the 4-inch edge and sew a 1/2-inch seam. (See Figure 5.3.)

Step 2: Attach strip 3 to the remaining raw edge of strip 2.

Step 3: Open the seams and press flat.

Step 4: Turn in the top and bottom raw edges 1/4 inch and press. Fold the edges 1/4 inch once again and press.

Step 5: Fold and press the side edges as above.

Step 6: Topstitch a narrow hem around all four sides. (To create pointed sash ends, see directions for the basic waist apron tie variation, page 21.) Set aside.

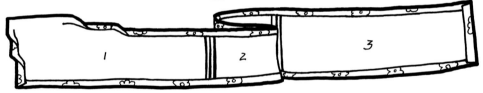

Figure 5.3

STORE BROWN SUGAR in the freezer to prevent hardening. To soften hardened brown sugar, pop it in the fridge for a few days.

To edge the apron

Step 1: Match the raw edges of the fabric with the right side of the bias tape and pin in place. (See Figure 5.4.)

Step 2: Sew all around the apron edges.

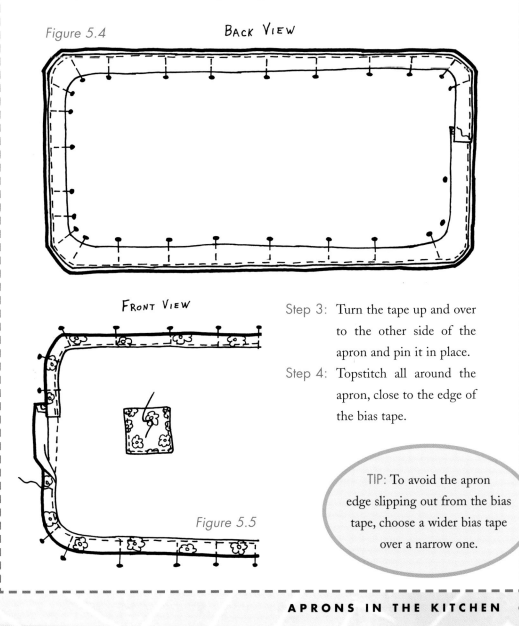

Figure 5.4

BACK VIEW

FRONT VIEW

Figure 5.5

Step 3: Turn the tape up and over to the other side of the apron and pin it in place.

Step 4: Topstitch all around the apron, close to the edge of the bias tape.

TIP: To avoid the apron edge slipping out from the bias tape, choose a wider bias tape over a narrow one.

For the pocket

Step 1: Pin together the two 5-inch pocket squares so the right sides are facing each other. (See Figure 5.6.) Starting on the bottom, stitch around the entire square 1/2 inch from the edge, leaving a 1/2-inch opening at the bottom in order to turn the pocket.

Step 2: Trim the corners as shown.

Step 3: Turn the pocket right side out, pushing it through the opening. Turn the raw edges back into the opening and press the entire pocket.

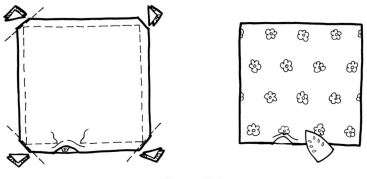

Figure 5.6

Step 4: Measure 3 inches down from the top edge of the skirt and 11 inches in from the right or left side. Pin your pocket here.

Step 5: Topstitch around the two sides and the bottom of the pocket. Backstitch at the beginning and end points to reinforce them.

DROP A LEMON into hot water for several minutes before squeezing to double the yield of lemon juice.

For the casing

Step 1: Turn in the top and bottom edges ¼ inch and press.

Step 2: At each end, turn in 1 inch and press.

Figure 5.7

BACK VIEW

Figure 5.8
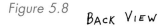

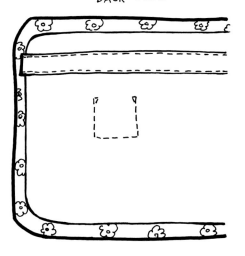

Step 3: On the back side of the apron, pin the casing to the apron 1½ inches down from the top edge of the apron, with the raw edges of the casing facing the back of the apron.

Step 4: Topstitch the top and bottom of the casing to the apron, leaving both ends open.

To pull the sash through the casing

Step 1:   Fold one end of the sash over the eraser end of a pencil or the rounded end of a knife and begin pushing this end through one
opening of the casing until it comes out the other end.

Step 2:   Grab this end of the sash and remove the pencil or knife.

Step 3:   Pull the sash through the casing, taking care that the sash doesn't
twist inside the casing.

Step 4:   Gather the apron along the sash.

CORRECT OVERSALTED SOUP by dropping large slices of raw potato into the soup pot and boiling for a short time. Then remove all of the potato, which will have absorbed most of the salt.

VARIATION: Make a matching set of a basic waist apron and child's apron by using leftover fabric from the basic waist apron for the child's sash and pocket.

every apron tells a story
Rob Miketa

I am the private chef to a family who requires my services during the holidays, when they entertain with large, lavish parties. This means I'm rarely able to spend holidays with my own family, which makes whenever I can get home a celebration of sorts.

Home is a farmhouse built in 1948 by my grandparents. Growing up, I spent so much time in this old kitchen. While my cousins were out playing, I was inside with my grandmothers, learning to cook the old-fashioned way—everything made from scratch and always made with love.

The cobbler-style apron I wore as a kid was the extra one every kitchen had for someone to lend a helping hand. I remember it to this day because it was made out of polyester and was a noisy jumble of hideous colors. My professional apron is just the opposite—crisp, white, and linen—and when I'm cooking a special dinner when I'm back home with my family, that's the one I tie on. Then I slip off my shoes to cook, something I only do when I'm with family. Walking barefoot over the old kitchen floor reminds me of those days when I was the student and my grandmothers, in their funny, colorful old aprons, were the real chefs.

Misses' Cobbler Apron
Easily Made

McCall's
PRINTED PATTERN *with* TRANSFER

1713

BLUE

SIZE
LARGE
18-20

25¢

A

B

B

CHILL CANDLES IN the refrigerator for twenty-four hours before using so they will burn evenly without dripping.

chapter 4

ALL AROUND THE HOUSE

❀

THE APRON reminds us of a way-back-when day when housework was truly a hands-on affair—washing dishes, dusting, vacuuming, laundry, ironing—these were the nuts and bolts of keeping a home tidy and clean. Not very glamorous, though, and decidedly lacking in glory. Who, after all, gets high fives for a well-washed load of laundry or kudos for an expertly dusted room? Generations of women have called housekeeping "drudgery," even today with our smart appliances, high-tech gadgety doodads, and space-age products. I prefer to take the Zen approach to housework, keeping it simple and mindful, and occasionally doing it the old-fashioned way. After all, as sophisticated as that top-of-the-line digitized clothes dryer might be, can it beat the smell of bed sheets dried outside on the line on a bright spring day? Never.

To accommodate its myriad tasks and responsibilities, the around-the-house apron often features generous sized pockets that are like mini-Dumpsters to fill with the flotsam and jetsam of daily living—grocery lists, phone messages, pencil stubs, Legos, paper clips, pet chewies, and loose change from under the seat cushions of the family room couch. These kangaroo pockets act as catchalls as you move from room to room and chore to chore, or to carry the tools of your labor at the ready.

An item could get lost once dropped into the giant pocket of a smock apron (also known as a "cobbler's apron") from these 1950s patterns.

every apron tells a story

Susan Keller

I was first married in June 1967, two days before my college graduation from Stanford University. I hadn't gotten into the performing arts graduate school I was interested in, so getting married seemed like the right thing to do.

Inspired by the thick horn-rimmed glasses of my intended, an owl theme pervaded our wedding gifts—we received several owl-adorned serving trays, a set of owl highball glasses, owl hand towels, and even an owl

ice bucket, an entertaining essential! Some years later, I received an owl apron and pot holders from my grandmother, who seemed not to have noticed that I'd been divorced from the man whose glasses inspired all the owl gifts in the first place. Long after all the highball glasses were broken and my ex had moved on, I still wear this apron for the large family dinners I love to host.

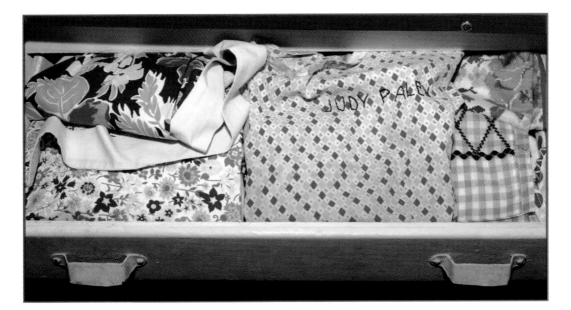

SMALL LOADS OF laundry dry at a lower heat setting and in less time than large loads.

Identified not by their jobs but by their wearers, *mekhuteneste* aprons, from the Yiddish for "mother of my son-in-law" or "mother of my daughter-in-law" featured brightly colored fabrics with contrasting trim, signature patterns that were like a family's kitchen coat of arms. Here, Judy Paley's faded *mekhuteneste*, made by her Hungarian grandmother and embroidered by Judy in a junior high home ec class.

Every homemaker used to have aprons specific to the week's chores—a wash-day apron, a housework apron, a gardening apron, and so on—a drawerful of aprons for every task. "Company aprons" might be pressed and folded at the back of the apron drawer, while everyday aprons were kept handy at the front. Many a bride's trousseau contained fine handmade aprons for every occasion, from an every-night supper apron to an everyday cleaning apron to an apron to be worn exclusively for serving cocktails.

One of my favorite task aprons is one sewn of soft towel terry that is worn during baby bath time, and is used to scoop up, wrap, and dry a freshly bathed baby. Hardly a chore at all! Try this simple variation on a bib apron, which makes a great new baby gift, too.

The Baby Bath Wrapper

Sew the apron body of a basic bib apron (see page 31) out of 12-ounce terry cloth, which is the weightier terry used for those delicious plush robes provided by spas. Turn leftover terry into a matching bath mitt by edging the wrapper and mitt in the same binding, following the edging instructions from the basic child's apron on page 63.

every apron tells a story
Ronnie Crawford

Mom had aprons for every occasion, and on wash day, she wore a magic apron, or so I thought when I was four. Every Monday, Mom had a wash-day ritual. We had an agitator washer with a wringer on top. After washing the clothes, she would crank each piece through the wringer and then it would drop into a fabric-lined basket. When the basket was filled, she'd tie on her magic apron and, motioning me to follow her, she'd carry the basket outside to the clothesline. After cleaning the line with a damp rag, she'd start hanging the laundry.

With one hand holding the clothing to the line, she'd dip her hand into the apron's pocket and pull out a clothespin. I'd watch her hang basket after basket and never run out of clothespins. It was like magic to me how her apron pocket always seemed to stay full.

Freshly Pressed

Since an entire day was once required to hand wash and dry the week's laundry, wash day and ironing day were never on the same day. Which is just as well, because ironing is its own fine art, as any great ironer will tell you. For those for whom ironing is the ultimate chore, the invention of miracle fibers in the 1950s and the ensuing decades of textile improvement changed everything. Now clothing whipped straight from the dryer to the hanger needs little or no pressing. A boon to all but those who love to iron!

Everything in Its Place

You can say what you want about housework—dusting, vacuuming, mopping, and so forth—but besides having dinner together every night, there's nothing more valuable to a household than order. A tidy home provides structure for family life and an oasis from the chaos of daily living. And these sorts of household chores keep us in touch with our possessions, ideally in a constant state of measuring their value in our lives. Housekeeping chores are *made* for divvying up among family members—cleaning gets done more quickly, everyone is invested in the care of the home, and good habits are established and shared all the way around.

That said, white-glove dust tests and the like have no place in busy, happy homes. Schedule the top-to-bottom, inside-out housecleaning for twice a year, in springtime, and then again in the fall. And in the meantime, just be systematic and efficient, addressing a small handful of straightforward chores every day (say, kitchen and bathroom cleanup, and a daily sweep for surface clutter) and keeping larger chores few and simple and less frequent (dusting, vacuuming, or laundry, for example).

The efficient way to go about cleaning a room is to start at the top and work your way down. Dust or vacuum the highest corners of the ceiling for cobwebs, and then the tops of curtain rods, window ledges, moldings, picture frames, ceiling fans, and light fixtures. This begins moving dust and dirt down to the floor, where you'll collect it all in a final, thorough vacuuming. Continue working downward, dusting shelves, books and objects from the highest spots down to the

SHARPEN SCISSORS BY cutting a piece of sandpaper once or twice.

every apron tells a story

Mary Wagner

As the oldest daughter in a family of six, I was ordained to help with the ironing. I started out ironing my mother's aprons, practicing first on the most stained and worn apron "just in case." Ironing, I learned, had rules. You always began with the waistband (which never seemed to lay flat) and then moved on to the pleats. I loved sliding my little needle-nosed iron into each hidden crevice. Next were the pockets, often the most challenging to iron, and then came the ties. Oh, how long you had to plead with them to stay put on the board. The detail ironing didn't bother me, because I knew that once the preliminary work was done, there came the reward of sliding my trusty iron over the limitless expanse of skirt.

Ironing became my bliss; I could take all the time I wanted and no one bothered me. When the first apron was ironed to my satisfaction, I would go to the refrigerator and choose another. I knew the best pieces were the ones hand-sprinkled at least a day before and rolled up tightly just so and left to chill.

> CONSIDER REPURPOSING,
> STORING, or discarding objects
> you repeatedly dust or polish
> but don't use.

lowest, including windowsills, lamps and tabletops, using cotton rags spritzed with your favorite all-purpose cleaner or furniture polish. When you've cleaned all surfaces and objects, give a quick vacuum of the furniture (on which some dust from above has likely fallen) and then vacuum the floor of the room from the corner furthest from the doorway, backing toward the door as your final destination. Done!

Carry a lightweight caddy of cleaning supplies from room to room. Better yet, wear a cobbler's apron with rags in one pocket and your cleaning supplies in each of the others. Or sew sturdy fabric hooks to the waistband of a waist or bib apron to keep your rags and spray bottles handy, gunslinger-style.

Three-Pocket Housework Apron

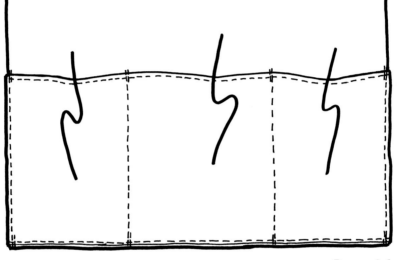

Figure 6.1

*T*urning any waist or smock apron into a three-pocket housework helper is a cinch. You will need a 10-inch piece of fabric that is the width of your apron skirt plus 1 inch. This piece is your pocket band. Turn the top edge of this fabric under 1/4 inch and press. Turn the fabric 1/4 inch once more, press, and sew a narrow top-stitch hem along the edge. Turn the other three edges over 1/2 inch and press. Pin the band to the skirt at the edges and topstitch along the two sides and the bottom. Decide how wide you want the pockets and pin to mark. Stitch from the top to the bottom at the marks to create the pockets, backstitching at the beginning and end of each row of stitching to reinforce.

Bedtime Story

Considering how much time we spend in our bed, it's amazing how little attention we pay to its care. There are three good rules for basic bed care that will make your sleeping environment more restful and healthy.

1. Keep your mattress clean. Scrub stains with an all-purpose cleanser. If you're mattress-stain prone, consider covering your mattress with a good-quality washable all-cotton mattress pad.

2. Clean under the bed. A dust ruffle seems like a nice idea, but really it's just in cahoots with the unhealthy stuff residing under your bed. Thoroughly vacuum weekly behind this skirt of deceptivity or just plain eliminate it.

3. Wash your bedclothes and redress your bed once a week like clockwork.

CLEANING RAGS SHOULD be made of 100 percent cotton. The best are cut from old flannel shirts, sweatshirts, undershirts, towels, flannel sheets, or—if you're lucky enough to have them— old-fashioned cloth baby diapers.

Amy Winger remembers a well-worn apron her grandmother donned to do her daily chores. Her most vivid memory is the very particular way her grandma made a bed. Below, Grandma Elvina's recipe for a comfortable bed:

Order a medium thickness egg foam pad from Sears, double up a thick wool Army blanket, and pull the bottom sheet taut across the whole thing. Then sprinkle a little loose Avon powder (any flowerly one will do) and rub it into the sheet.

You can picture this sweet halter-style bib apron on a bevy of homemaking heroines from the golden age of television, from Donna Stone to June Cleaver to Harriet Nelson. Why, even Lucy Ricardo might wear this, tidying up her apartment while undoing the day's disaster.

"Mother's Apron"

There's a great old skit called "Mother's Apron" that touts the many household uses of the apron. This basic skit, with its infinite individual variations, has been performed by women's church and community clubs for generations. Below is a version remembered by Bernice Esau that was presented by her mother, probably originally in Low German, the common language of the rural Minnesota community where it was performed, hence the slightly lilting, old-fashioned sound to it:

Do you remember Mother's aprons? Always big they were, and their uses were many. Besides the foremost purpose, the protection of the dress beneath, it was a holder for removal of hot pans from the oven. It was wonderful for drying children's tears and, yes, even for wiping small noses. From the henhouse it carried eggs, fuzzy chicks, ducklings, or goslings, and sometimes half-hatched eggs to be finished in the warming oven. Its folds provided an ideal hiding place for shy children, and when guests lingered on chilly days, the apron was wrapped about Mother's arms. Innumerable times it wiped a perspiring brow bent over a hot wood-burning stove. Corncobs and wood kindlings came to the kitchen stove in that ample garment, as did fresh peas and string beans from the garden. Often they were podded and stemmed in the lap the apron covered. Windfall apples were gathered in it, and wildflowers. Chairs were hastily dusted with its corners when unexpected company was sighted. Waving it aloft was as good as a dinner bell to call the men from the field. Big they were, and useful. Now I wonder, will any modern-day apron provoke such sweet and homesick memories?

> GLASSES THAT ARE stuck together can be separated without breaking by putting cold water in the top glass and setting the bottom glass in warm water.

chapter 5

BACKYARD DADDY

❁

MY SONS tell me I have a selective memory when it comes to my stories of growing up in the fabulous, fun-filled 1950s. Of course, they're a little bit right about that, but what's absolutely genuine are the memories I have of my own Backyard Daddy.

Back then, everyone's daddy was king of the backyard, wearing a goofy apron and chef's hat, sipping a can of something cool, and flicking cigarette ashes while flipping burgers on a charcoal grill. There's something perfectly contemporary about that image, too, though today's Backyard Daddy is more likely sipping a designer brew through a slice of lemon and carefully turning a spice-rubbed salmon fillet on a high-tech gas grill.

> *LABEL SEPARATE TRASH bins for garbage and recyclables.*

Nothing chronicles a man's love affair with the barbecue grill over the years like the wonderful aprons I have collected, especially the old-timey, slightly grimy, short-order cook-style chef aprons, decorated with dancing hot dogs and grinning hamburgers and a "Tip the Cook" pocket. The mock formal styles mimicking a butler's uniform or a tuxedo, the funny modern "message" aprons that say things like "Kiss the Chef," "Charred and Dangerous," and "License to Grill," and the risqué with a surprise for anyone daring enough to lift the appliquéd apron-on-apron—it's all humor to grill for. These clever male aprons imply that for Mom, in her everyday apron, cooking was a chore. But for the Backyard Daddy at the grill, it is all about having a good time.

It *is* good fun to eat off of paper plates and lick savory sauce off your fingers and spit watermelon seeds onto the grass. So hand your man his apron, a refreshing beverage, and a stack of franks and burgers to pile on the grill. Who's cooking now?

Early men's aprons ranged from the serious, as with the Simplicity pattern for an apron that really wants to be a business suit (above), to the silly, as with this "in the doghouse" husband apron.

every apron tells a story

Nancy Foster

My dad, Asa B. Foster, was born in 1911 and was definitely a graduate of the school of hard knocks. He was orphaned at sixteen, but went on to make a good life for himself and his family. Some years ago, I went back to clean out my childhood home and discovered a collection of aprons, including the chef outfit on the next page that was my dad's. He'd wear it at family and neighborhood events, especially during the summer. Dad loved making condiments, and this apron is stained with one of his specialties: a great sweet and spicy barbecue sauce.

Asa Foster's Finger-Lickin', Butt-Kickin' Barbecue Sauce

2 tablespoons vegetable oil

$1/2$ cup finely chopped onion

2 teaspoons minced garlic

$2/3$ cup cider vinegar

One 8-ounce can tomato sauce

$1/4$ cup tightly packed brown sugar

1 tablespoon dry mustard

1 teaspoon chili powder

1 teaspoon salt

1 teaspoon hot sauce

$1/4$ teaspoon freshly ground black pepper

SOAK WOODEN SKEWERS in water for twenty minutes before threading with food to prevent burning and food sticking to the skewers.

FILL A BASKET with a selection of mosquito repellant, including a natural citronella cream, along with a pop-up canister of wet handwipes.

Heat the vegetable oil in a 1-quart saucepan over medium heat. Add the onions and garlic to the pan and cook, stirring often, until softened, 3 to 4 minutes. Add the vinegar to the pan and cook for 2 minutes. Place the remainder of the ingredients in the saucepan and bring to a simmer. Cook the sauce for 20 minutes or so, until it thickens, and remove from the heat. Cool completely, then transfer to a glass or plastic container and refrigerate until ready to use. Slather on chicken or chops on the grill and serve a little extra at the table. The sauce will keep in the refrigerator for 2 weeks. Makes 1$\frac{1}{2}$ cups.

All the accoutrements of the backyard barbecue appeal to me. In particular, setting a table with a vintage tablecloth, partaking of those divine mayonnaise-y potluck dishes you'd never make for yourself, and the aforementioned disposable paper plates. And dressing cola or brew or wine bottles in their own irresistible aprons. Adorable, of course, and a cinch to make.

SECURE TABLECLOTHS WITH clothespins at strategic spots around the table to prevent a breeze from lifting the cloth.

The Bottle Apron

To dress a bottle in a chef-style bib apron, you will need paper, scissors, a ruler, scrap fabric, and 2 feet of ribbon. To draw the pattern, measure and outline a rectangle 6 inches tall and 5 inches wide on a piece of paper. Cut out along your measuring lines. Fold the paper in half. At the top edge, mark 1 inch from the fold. From this point, mark 2½ inches down. Now mark 1½ inches to the paper's edge. Draw a line connecting these marks.

Cut out the pattern; it should look like a mini chef's apron. Place your fabric right side up, lay the pattern on it, and cut out the little apron. Pink the raw edges or fold the edges and topstitch. Fold the piece of ribbon in half lengthwise to mark the center. Measure 3 inches from the center on both sides and mark. Pin the ribbon to the bib's left and right top edges; this is the bottle's neck loop. Topstitch the ribbon to the edges of the apron's bib, leaving 6 inches unattached at each end for the apron's ties.

To feminize, round the corners and edge in eyelet, rickrack, or gathered lace. Purchased chef aprons can be customized to match the bottlewear and packaged as a hospitality gift in lieu of flowers.

every apron tells a story

Erin McDaniels Owens

My ancestral roots run deep through the South, and in New Orleans, Nanny and Grammy, my great-grandmother and grandmother, are still remembered as good cooks and gracious hostesses. Their specialty was classic Southern food, and in particular, the use of Coca-Cola in many dishes. In their day, Coke was a pantry staple, as much an ingredient of the dishes they were famous for as it was for its restorative properties.

Every day in late afternoon, Nanny and Grammy dressed my mother and her siblings in fresh clothes and sent them to the veranda to wait for their father's return home for dinner. While they waited, they sipped Cokes from bottles dressed in tiny aprons. Handmade by Nanny and Grammy, each apron was trimmed in a white ruffle and rick-rack, and on the front was stitched a minuscule pocket to hold a paper straw. In today's world, the notion of these precious aprons might appear ridiculous to most people. But to me, the gentility of the gesture speaks to the days when husbands returned home after a hard day's work to a family eager to greet him.

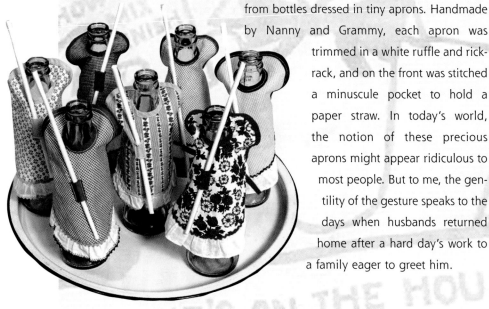

As my mother's only daughter, I inherited her cherished Southern traditions, her collection of bottle aprons, and all her secret recipes featuring Coke as an ingredient. To this day, I still pour the sweet syrupy liquid over my ham before baking, and nothing tastes as good as Coke and Cherry Jell-O Salad.

Coke and Cherry Jell-O Salad

Mix together an 8-ounce can of drained crushed pineapple, a can of drained Bing cherries, and $1/2$ cup of chopped pecans. Spread this mixture across the bottom of a 9 x 13-inch pan. Dissolve 2 small boxes of cherry flavored Jell-O in 2 cups of boiling water. Stirring gently, pour a 12-ounce can of ice cold Coke into the Jell-O. Pour this mixture over the fruit mixture and chill until firm.

Makes 10-12 servings.

SPRAY GRILL RACKS with nonstick spray before lighting or igniting the grill.

DAD TOOK grilling seriously, and he was totally in charge of whatever he was cooking on the grill, especially his signature hamburgers. His recipe included a particular mix of ground beef, crushed crackers, eggs, and herbs that he grew in his garden. The ingredients were blended by hand, and the mixture yielded eight burgers per pound of beef. Dad grilled several nights a week, making dinner a lively main event. Donning his chef's apron and hat, he'd load up the grill with burgers, and while they cooked, he'd serenade us with his harmonica.

—Gina Marie Hayworth

Today's Backyard Dad

Today's state-of-the-art grill-meister might be found wearing a professional chef's apron, searing and simmering and slathering with sophisticated seasonings and sauces. Our backyard dad is swiftly becoming less of a burger flipper and more of a connoisseur, and he's discovering the grill as an outlet for creative cookery. Blame those hot dog chefs on television for daring us to cook anything we can think of on a grill.

EASY
GRILLED PIZZA

A BALL of ready-made refrigerated or frozen dough from the grocery store. Jarred sauces of your choice, including Alfredo, tomato, or herbed olive oil. Toppings such as favorite varieties of shredded cheese, chopped peppers and onions, mushrooms, spinach, sliced tomato, avocado, pepperoni, crumbled sausage, or shrimp.

Cut your dough into four equal pieces, then let them rise in bowls for 20 minutes in a warm spot loosely covered by a damp cloth. Meanwhile, precook the veggie, meat, or fish toppings and prepare your grill.

Clean your grill well to remove the flavors and residue of recently grilled food. Brush the grill surface with oil or spray with olive oil or nonstick spray. Heat the grill to a nice medium heat.

Roll out each piece of dough on a floured surface for individual-sized pizzas. Transfer the dough to the grill and cook until it just begins to bake, then turn. Grill for several minutes more, adding toppings for the last 2 or 3 minutes. Take care that the bottom of the crust doesn't burn.

TURN FOODS USING a different spatula, tongs, or fork than you used to first place food on the grill to avoid transferring bacteria the uncooked food might have harbored.

Pizzas can be removed from the grill temporarily after turning so guests can arrange their own toppings. Then the pizzas can be returned to the grill to finish.

chapter 6

MAID IN AMERICA:
APRONS ON THE JOB

❀

PROFESSIONAL CHEFS aren't the only ones who get to wear an apron to work. There are welders and farriers and fishmongers and printers and grocery clerks and artists and florists and bakers and housekeepers and lab technicians and carpenters, to name a few who call an apron their uniform, and lucky them. How nice to be able to shift gears from leisure to work and back again with the tug of an apron string. The late couture fashion designer Geoffrey Beene wore a smock on the job for more than forty years for exactly that reason, to plug into his work each morning by donning his smock, and to unplug by hanging it back up on its hook at the end of the day. What a lovely ritual.

WHISTLE WHILE YOU work. It really does make a difference.

The rest of us wear aprons to work to let people know we are working and, of course, to keep our clothes clean. Some of my favorite aprons in my collection are the ones that proudly show the honest, hard work of the person who wore it—a frayed but crisply ironed waitress apron, a beautician's smock colorfully smeared with hair dyes, and the bleached white of a butcher's bib.

ALWAYS TIP THE hotel maid; hers is the only hand that's not outstretched and the only hand that cleans up after you.

A SMILE TRANSLATES *even over the phone, so before answering its ring, take a breath and smile.*

BACK WHEN my grandpa opened Whitman Drugstore in 1904, ointments and medications were mixed right on the spot, as were the sodas at the fountain. During junior high and high school, I worked the fountain counter and wore the apron and paper hat that was the uniform of a soda jerk, so-called because of the quick motion required to dispense just the right amount of syrup and carbonated water to make a soda. As head soda jerk, I would scoop extra ice cream into my friends' milkshakes, and if I was sweet on a girl, she'd get an extra cherry on her hot fudge sundae.

—Neil Whitman

Harold Sasaki

M y grandmother Sasaki's apron was her purse, and she wore it all the time. It was quite plain, full-length, with crossed straps in the back and front pockets, which always held Bull Durham tobacco, cigarette paper, and matches. She rolled her own cigarettes, so her fingers were stained brown from the tobacco—not exactly a ladylike image, but she smoked like a lady, taking tiny puffs of her cigarette.

Bachan (the Japanese word for grandmother) Kimi was born in Japan, a country where the firstborn male was like a king and made choices for the entire family. An obedient wife, *Bachan* worked in her husband's family's poi manufacturing business in Kona, Hawaii, sewing, washing, and darning the poi bags. Although the men managed the business, my *bachan* was very smart. When she spoke her mind, she said important things about life, like "Use money, don't let it use you." Or "Those parents are too sharp," which meant that parents who do too much for a child end up with a child who doesn't have the tools to figure out life. *Bachan's* gems were so wise, we called them "pearly wisdoms."

My *bachan* was wise, but my mother was wiser, my wife even wiser, and my daughter the wisest of them all. She carries with her the traits of the three most important women in my life, strong women who worked hard and left a legacy of their wisdom for her; she is insightful, determined, and mentally tough.

A PICTURE postcard circa early 1930s of a cheerful group of aproned workers at a camp in Longmont, Colorado. According to the person who wrote the postcard, left to right, that's Dishwasher Charlie, Eunice, Boss, Mary, Dorothy, and Cook Andy. The postcard's author, not named, is the young lady third from the left and standing on the ground. She wrote: "Our gang out at the dining hall. They are a jolly bunch and heaps of fun."

The Wipe-and-Go Plastic Apron

To make this utterly practical apron, rustle up a colorful vinyl picnic tablecloth, preferably the kind with a soft flannel-like backing. Spread the tablecloth out on a flat surface and cut out the shape of a basic waist apron (see page 17), as well as two strips for waist ties and a pocket. Follow the directions for constructing the waist apron. The best part? You just clean it with a damp sponge!

AN APRON DOUBLES as a hand towel, never as a tissue.

This plastic apron was made of Koroseal, an early BF Goodrich flexible material.

The beauty parlor used to be a woman's weekly destination for companionship, gossip, advice, and a hair set and manicure. As the hairdresser deftly rotated her customers from one station to the next, her plastic apron protected her clothing from soaks and stains, with the pocket as her bank. What a good idea!

every apron tells a story

Wilhelmenia Brown

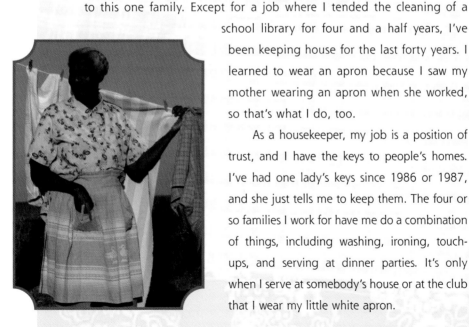

I was born in Charleston, South Carolina. I wasn't exactly expected because my mother thought she was through, you know. My parents had already named thirteen or so children and they just ran out, so they let the insurance man pick my name.

My father was a mattress maker and my mother was a housekeeper to this one family. Except for a job where I tended the cleaning of a school library for four and a half years, I've been keeping house for the last forty years. I learned to wear an apron because I saw my mother wearing an apron when she worked, so that's what I do, too.

As a housekeeper, my job is a position of trust, and I have the keys to people's homes. I've had one lady's keys since 1986 or 1987, and she just tells me to keep them. The four or so families I work for have me do a combination of things, including washing, ironing, touch-ups, and serving at dinner parties. It's only when I serve at somebody's house or at the club that I wear my little white apron.

every apron tells a story

Jean Rather

No sunbonnet for her, but like her grandmother, artist Jean Rather wouldn't dream of working without wearing an apron.

My grandmother's family left Europe and moved to Central Texas in 1854. Texas was truly wild at that time, especially compared to their former home near Dresden, Germany. My grandmother was born into the starkness of the land as it was back then, and by the time I was born, her life was perfectly symbolized by her uniform—a sunbonnet and an apron sewn out of a flour sack.

From early morning to after dark, she worked hard. She managed a family, and in sandy, sunbaked dirt, grew a garden that yielded the vegetables she'd cook for the noon meal, often for as many as a dozen. On an unmarked gravel road, she operated the only country store within fifteen miles of there, and in her apron pockets, she carried penny candies she gave out to the children of laborers.

My grandmother grew white roses, played the pump organ, raised three sons, and lost her only daughter as a baby, who died after she ate poison berries. If I were to paint her, she'd appear as I remember her— wearing a sunbonnet and an apron.

Hank Geisel

I am the only child of Holocaust sur-
vivors. My father was a demanding, dif-
ficult person, and my mother was just
the opposite—gentle and loving, totally dependent, and always a bit bewil-
dered. Their marriage was brokered by
siblings who made it to the United
States before them. My folks were so
mismatched. About the only thing they
had in common was me and their
dream that I be successful. The pressure
of being their Great Hope was hard on
me, but I managed. I got those top
grades they cared so much about and
most days after school, I helped out at
their business, Al's Market.

When I walked into the store after
school, the first thing I'd do was get a
large Pepsi and a Moon Pie or a
Snowball from the display rack. Getting

In 1939, Hank Geisel's father
(left, wearing an army-issue
cook's apron) was released from
Dachau and got out of Germany
just in time. Three years later, he
was stationed in France as a
sergeant in the U.S. Army.
Wearing that cook's apron as an
American citizen was the happi-
est time of his life.

to eat that junk for free was certainly the best part of my job there and
probably one of the highlights of my childhood. After my snack, I'd put on

a white butcher's apron that was identical to the aprons my parents were wearing, and I'd carry customers' bags out to their cars. I remember being so proud because I was helping out and in those days, people tipped the bag boy, so I made a little spending money, too.

If I were to choose a symbol for survival, a white butcher's apron would be one I'd consider. It defines my parents' work ethic and their deep desire to be productive citizens of America.

Put Your Feet Up Stew

In my opinion, one of the great inventions of all time for the workers of the world is the slow cooker or crockpot. After a long day on the job, nothing beats opening the door to a home that smells like dinner.

Layer the following ingredients in a crockpot:

3 medium-sized peeled potatoes, cut into bite-sized cubes

1 sliced beef sausage or keilbasa

2 (14$\frac{1}{2}$-ounce) cans cut green beans, drained

1 small onion, chopped

2 (10-ounce) cans cream of mushroom soup

1 cup shredded Cheddar cheese

Cook on low for 4 to 10 hours. Serve with a salad and warmed rolls or flour tortillas.

Feeds a hungry family of four.

chapter 7

JINGLE BELLE: APRONS FOR THE HOLIDAYS, ENTERTAINING, AND SPECIAL OCCASIONS

❀

NOTHING DRESSES up for a fancy to-do like an apron. It's like it puts on its lipstick and a slick pair of heels and it's ready to party! It's all flirt and flounce and Sunday best. Special-occasion aprons are just plain fun, from cheerful holiday confections to a lacy wisp for a cocktail party to tiers of flocked organza.

Take this holiday apron, one of my favorites. I love the luxe red satin material of the apron and the clever little candy cane

A TABLE DRESSED in wonderful linens is its own centerpiece.

This unique reversible holiday apron from my collection is very special to me. It was the first shared with me by a contributor, who wanted to be sure this extraordinary specimen would find an appreciative audience, which it certainly has!

Holidays beg for you to pull your special aprons
from the back of the drawer and dress festive.

ornaments all over it. And what about the little champagne glass doodad you can replace the ornaments with for New Year's Eve? Irresistible! This apron inspires all manner of variations for other holidays or celebrations—why not tiny jack o' lanterns and black cats adorning a Halloween apron, or leprechauns and clover for St. Paddy's Day? If you think of your apron as a blank canvas, you can dream up the most creative ways to fill it for any occasion.

every apron tells a story

Beth Richardson

Until my generation, aprons were so much a part of their everyday wardrobe that the women in my family didn't consider themselves dressed until they tied on their aprons. When my daughters were four and six years old, my mom sent them these darling teddy bear aprons as Christmas gifts. Morgan and Mallory loved them—I think because they knew the aprons were gifts from their grandma's heart.

I keep these aprons safely packed away and bring them out just once a year, at Christmas, when I integrate them into my holiday decorating. What's funny is that the only time of year I wear an apron myself is when I'm dressing the house for the holidays. The apron I wear belonged to my grandmother and is made of a Christmas print, complete with red bow and rick-rack. When I wear it, I feel a sentimental pull to my grandmother. I have two aprons that belonged to her that I plan to give to my daughters. I hope when my girls are grown they will feel the connection to the women in my family when they tie their own apron strings.

The 1950s were such a heyday of home entertainment. Neighborhood cocktail gatherings, dress-up dinner parties, bridge club get-togethers—all were the best kinds of excuses to get dolled up with your loveliest apron-wear. These aprons were more about the fluff and the flounce than they were about protecting one's clothing.

These are wonderful examples of daytime entertaining aprons, perfect for a tea in the garden or a game of cards with the girls.

The all-stars of the golden age of homemaking really knew how to put on the dog. It was not unusual to see aprons carefully coordinated with a tablecloth or cloth napkins for a special occasion. What a fun idea! Next time you have a special gathering in your home—a birthday luncheon or a wedding shower—use all your apron powers to make your party memorable.

The Apron
and Table Linen
Luncheon Ensemble

This cheerful ensemble was made from an old tablecloth,
one of the best ways I can think of to take something old
and wonderful and make it new and wonderful.

To create an entertainment ensemble, you will need a tablecloth to use as fabric for your apron and accessories. A tablecloth with an overall design provides the most pattern-cutting options, versus one with just a border design. Turning the tablecloth on the diagonal best utilizes its yardage. Stains can be cut around. Cut out the apron body of your choice. If there isn't enough fabric for a whole apron, use it for the pockets and ties or waistband. Use the remaining tablecloth to make placemats and coordinating napkins. Leftover strips of tablecloth can be trimmed with pinking shears and sewn together to become a ribbon. To create a matching gift card, iron a tablecloth scrap onto a piece of craft-weight Wonder Under paper-backed fusible web and cut the scrap into fun shapes. Peel the fusible paper from the back of the cut shape and iron it onto the front of a piece of 16- to 20-pound card stock.

ARRANGE VOTIVE CANDLES at each place setting to give every guest a flattering glow.

FOR THIRTY years, my mother had a weekly afternoon bridge date with the same group of three ladies—Gladys Burris, Terza Brown, and Laura Conroy. When it was Mother's turn to hostess, she wore a dressy little apron.
—Tom Jones

The hand-painted flowers on the pocket of this taffeta waist apron make it the fairest of the fair.

I love some of the handiwork in aprons people wear to entertain; you can see fabulous eye-catching detail and a real appreciation for what dressing up really means. Even a homemaker with limited means could invest time in making her "for company" aprons special. Elegant trim, intricate embroidery, and other festive flourishes jazzed up even the humblest hostess apron.

These vintage crocheted hostess aprons are almost too
pretty to wear, especially when you might—just might—
drip or spill a little something on them.

Party Like It's 1955

I can't think of a better way of bringing a
little of the fun-loving formality of 1950s-style
entertaining home than to throw a 1950s-style dinner party. Encourage your guests to
dress like the classic suburban characters from their favorite 1950s television shows. Ladies
in aprons, of course. Answer the doorbell together in matching host and hostess aprons.
Serve old-school mixed drinks like a Tom Collins or an old-fashioned, and pass retro hors
d'oeuvres, like pimento cheese on white bread triangles or pigs in a blanket. Your guests
will be dabbing their chins with their pencil-thin neckties and taffeta aprons when they
gobble up this vintage Chicken Olivia Casserole.

APRON-CLAD hostesses Eleanor Stiglitz Kornblueh and Edith Kornblueh Gekoski, Huntington, New York, 1953.

Chicken Olivia Casserole

2 cups pulled chicken

2 cups chopped celery

3 cups rice cooked in chicken stock

and a dash of tumeric for color

3/4 cup mayonnaise

2 tablespoons chopped onion

1 teaspoon lemon juice

1 teaspoon black pepper

2 hard-boiled eggs, chopped

1 cup chopped water chestnuts

1/2 10-ounce can cream of celery soup

1/2 10-ounce can cream of chicken soup

Mix all the ingredients together and spread in a greased 9 x 13-inch baking dish.

TOPPING:

1 stick butter ($^1/_4$ pound), melted
1 cup crushed cornflakes
$^1/_2$ cup sliced almonds
$^1/_2$ tablespoon dry parsley

Preheat oven to 350 degrees.

Mix the topping ingredients together. Top casserole with the topping mixture. Bake the casserole, uncovered, in the preheated oven for 40 minutes. This dish freezes well.

Makes 6 to 8 servings.

FREEZE LEFTOVER WINE into an ice cube tray and use to flavor sauces, gravies, and casseroles.

chapter 8

NOT YOUR GRANDMA'S APRON

❁

WHEN APRONS went mass market in the postwar boom of the late 1940s and 1950s, it was just a matter of time before they would reflect the zeitgeist of popular culture. The first signs of this came in the form of what I call "voice" aprons that spelled out actual messages, like a mirror of what people were thinking at the time. The messages might be sweet and simply homespun, as with "Expectant Mother." Or they might be funny, as with "Same Old Grind" or "The Honeymoon is Over." Sometimes they pointed to the frame of mind of the frustrated, increasingly vocal lady wearing the apron, who was probably wearing her "The Hell with Housework" apron the day she threw it down and got herself a job outside the home.

This playful
contemporary apron is
equal sizzle and smooch.

Aprons got to be sassier as the years passed, perhaps inspired by the image of the tan-
talizing chambermaid in her ruffled white bib and the like. It's as if the apron shifted from
functional to fun to fantasy and here we are, wearing aprons to play and flirt and tease. I
love wearing a classic apron to dress up my traditional side, and an offbeat design for my
kooky, fun lifestyle.

The "Me Jane" Apron

When you're not married to the conventional approach to aprons, the sky is the limit. Think of your apron as a costume and you could be swinging from the trees before you know it.

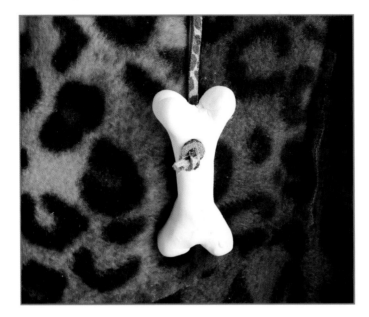

This little "wild thang" frolic is a snap to make. You will need: One 24 x 24-inch square of jungle print fleece, 2 yards of 1½-inch-wide ribbon, two bricks of white bakeable molding clay (each brick will make 4 to 5 bones), and 1 yard of skinny rawhide string or narrow ribbon.

Sew a double row of gathering stitches 1 inch from the top raw edge of the apron body, fitting and pinning the gathers to the ribbon. Topstitch along the ribbon's edges. Cut the apron's pocket and bottom hem jaggedy. Topstitch the pocket 4 inches from the top edge.

To make the bones, divide the clay and shape each portion to look like a bone. Use a large needle to poke a hole in each bone, then widen the holes a bit, as they will close somewhat during baking. Bake bones according to the package's instructions. When baked and cool, thread a leather strip or ribbon through the hole in each bone, tie a knot to secure, then sew the other end to your apron.

every apron tells a story
Linda Jaeger Laws

I grew up the only girl in a house full of boys, and while in someone else's house I might have been the princess, in our house, I was just one of the guys. I loved my lace socks and Mary Janes, but I also loved sharing

the chores, responsibilities, and challenges growing up with my three brothers. Given my upbringing, my fondness for aprons is ironic.

I have several aprons, including a childhood apron I'm very fond of and a few that remind me of the wonderful family gatherings orchestrated by my mother and grandmother. I tend to wear an apron myself, though, only when I'm in a particular sort of happy and sentimental mood. And when I am in this mood, I make pies.

The apron I wear is a long, delicately embroidered wispy apron my husband and I found at an estate sale. It had been wrapped in tissue for who knows how many years and it was in pristine condition. Up early, and while the rest of the house is still sleeping and no one is likely to appear at the door, it's this gauzy apron I don and, otherwise in the buff, bake pies.

I like to make my pies as appealing on the outside as they are delicious, so I use the top crust like a canvas, carving designs into one or sculpting ornamental figures for another with extra dough. As the rising sun lights up the sky, I line up my pies to cool on the back porch railing. Pie for breakfast—is there a more jubilant start to the day?

No-Mess Piecrust

1 cup flour

8 teaspoons vegetable oil

$1/4$ cup milk plus 1 teaspoon

$1/4$ teaspoon salt

1 teaspoon sugar

Preheat the oven to 400 degrees. Put all the ingredients in an ungreased 8-inch pie plate and mix everything together with your fingers or a fork. When the mixture is damp and starting to stick together, press the dough into the bottom of the pie plate and up the sides. Prick a few times with the tines of a fork. Bake in the preheated oven until golden brown. (8–10 minutes, maybe less depending on your oven. Better to bake just until the color is right.) Brush beaten egg white on the warm crust and cool. Fill with prepared instant chocolate pudding, chill in the refrigerator, for an hour and you've got pie! Top each serving with a dollop of whipped cream flavored with grated citrus peel, and you've got a slice of yum!

Makes 6 to 8 servings.

The Money Apron

Available in a rainbow of colors, tulle was easily stitched into aprons. Tulle aprons matching the mints served at weddings and showers were provided by the bride's mother and worn by her friends, who acted as helpers with such important duties as receiving line coordinator, guest book registrar, punch pourer, ribbon collector, and cookie platter arranger. A tulle apron can be embellished for any holiday or event with dabs of tacky glue and decorations appropriate to the theme, as well as provide a unique way to give a gift of cash.

YOU WILL NEED: 1½ yards of tulle for the apron's body, 1+ yard of grosgrain ribbon for the waistband and ties, and 4-inch strips of narrow satin ribbon to wrap the bills, thread, scissors, a pencil, and straight pins. Sew a double row of gathering stitches an inch or so below the top raw edge, fitting and pinning the gathers to the ribbon. Topstitch the ribbon to the tulle. Affix the ribbons with teeny safety pins. For a guy version, use strips of twill in place of the ribbons and a bistro or purchased chef-style apron.

AN APRON PARTY

MAKE A party all about the apron. Model your party after a quilting bee, and invite a crafty group of old friends and new acquaintances. For your apron-making fixin's, hit the fabric store for lots of inexpensive broadcloth and patterned fabrics, remnant bundles, and a selection of hem tape, rickrack, felt, buttons, or other decorative doodads. Precut the pattern pieces for simple waist aprons out of several different fabrics so your guests can mix and match. Set up your iron and your sewing machine with a bright, universally appealing color of thread, and take turns pressing and stitching together your aprons. If you've got a group of nonsewers, provide a batch of bright white chef's aprons, fabric markers, a glue gun, and a fun selection of decorative trimmings.

An apron-making party is adaptable to every imaginable celebration, from a baby or wedding shower to an anniversary to a family reunion. Set out one white chef's apron and ask your guests to contribute a bit of wit, wisdom, or creativity with a Sharpie or fabric markers. For a bridal shower, for instance, ask guests to write their best advice for a good marriage: "Don't go to bed mad," "Hold hands," or "Don't correct his table manners— he has a mother!"

I love the idea of a holiday apron created in this style. Next Thanksgiving, set out an apron with a bunch of colorful fabric markers and ask family and guests to write or draw something they're thankful for. Or to draw and label their favorite Thanksgiving dish. As the years pass, these aprons will become like a living scrapbook of those special gatherings.

Finally, how about creating a custom apron that *is* the invitation to your party? Write your invitation front and center on white chef's aprons:

Melissa and Steve's Surprise Housewarming
Saturday, June 1 at 6:00 p.m. at the M&S "Ranch"
Bring your favorite BBQ sauce and cookout recipe.

Roll the apron and tie with a colorful bandana, and don't be surprised if guests turn up wearing their own invitations.

VISIT SECONDHAND STORES around Halloween, when aprons are often spotted on the costume racks.

chapter 9

APRON MEMORIES

❁

I AM an apron collector. When I discover an apron with handiwork, my heart beats faster. I am awed by the delicate embroidery, clever original designs, and adornments. Less than perfect stitchery also leaves me palpitating, because given the odds, it is miraculous such delicacies survived. Preserving such beautiful work is the calling of an apron collector. As with any kind of collecting, there's some instinct and judgment involved in gathering worthy specimens, but with aprons, besides your good eye to guide you, you also have your heart whispering in your ear. With aprons, which are growing increasingly popular, you can build a wonderful collection using the Internet to access auctions and vintage clothing sites.

First, though, start right in your own home. Rummage in the attic. Ask older family members if they saved their aprons—and ask them for their apron stories while you're at it! Visit weekend estate sales, flea markets, yard sales, secondhand stores, and antique shops.

Whether embroidered free form or stitched within a prestamped design, aprons with embroidery work are historical artifacts as well as vintage domestic treasures. To minimize damage to embroidery, avoid direct application of the iron's heat to the threads, and use a press cloth as a buffer.

ASK YOUR LOCAL dry cleaner
if you can buy a bit of acid-free
tissue paper to use when folding
and storing your aprons.

Checked gingham provides a natural guide for cross-stitch. Any design will work, with the motif's size depending on the size of the checks. For a symmetrical appearance, place your design in the middle of your fabric, so you begin in the center and work outward. Cross-stitch may be worked from right to left or left to right, but it will look best when all the topstitches slant in the same direction; then work back over the topstitches in the opposite direction.

Collecting, Preserving, and Displaying Aprons

Remember that the aprons in your collection were sewn, purchased, or given as gifts with one purpose in mind—to be worn. And worn they were! I believe the best way to enjoy your collection is to wear it. Wear your most durable aprons the way they were meant to be worn: when you're cooking, cleaning, or otherwise living your life. Save your more delicate aprons for special occasions, to dress up for a holiday meal or to play hostess when entertaining. If you have a special apron that's just too fragile to wear, but you'd like to have it out for guests to appreciate and enjoy, hang it on a pretty hanger in a visible spot in your kitchen (well out of splatter's way, of course!).

If you must tuck your aprons away, here are some storage suggestions to minimize their wear and tear:

- Do not starch your aprons prior to storing them.
- Store your aprons flat, not folded. If you can't store them flat, the next best thing to do is to roll them. If you must fold your aprons, however, refold them at least twice a year, folded differently than they had previously been stored. Place acid-free tissue paper between each apron and use more when folding or rolling individual aprons.

Of the hundreds of aprons I own, this one from the early 1920s is the oldest, and to me, the most captivating. When I saw it in an Atlanta antiques store—with the embroidery perfectly stitched and painstakingly tiny, the sheer fabric the color of a girl's sweet blush, and the ribboned waistband with its satin rosettes—I *had* to have it.

- Apron fabric needs to breathe, so keep them in a drawer or in archival-quality storage boxes. Do not store the aprons in plastic bins or plastic bags.
- Use herbal moth repellents inside your storage drawers or boxes to keep away moths and other cloth-eating insects. Herb sachets need to be replaced every few months or reactivated with essential oils such as lavender and rosemary. Cedar blocks are also good protection.

Displaying Your Aprons

Aprons are textile artifacts and the age of each should be considered when planning to display them. One of my favorite ways to display a rare or fragile apron is to frame it. This protects your apron and turns it into a work of art. To frame an apron, follow these guidelines:

- Gently hand wash the apron to remove starch, stains, body oils, and old food crusties. (OxiClean and Orvis are two good products for laundering vintage textiles.) Soak the apron according to the instructions on the product label, and rinse until the water is completely clear. Try not to twist or wring the apron or hold it high out of its bath—the stress and weight of the wet fabric could damage the apron's design and cause small holes to become larger tears.
- Do not dry your aprons in the dryer. Drape them over a clothesline, indoors or out, or dry flat on a towel as with any delicate clothing.
- Whether you frame it yourself or hire a framer, be sure to use an acid-free mat board. Do not affix the apron to the board with glue; rather use pins or inconspicuous stitches.
- Use UV conservation clear glass, especially if it will be hung where there is fluorescent lighting or indirect sunshine. Otherwise, regular glass is fine. Use spacers to protect the apron from being pressed by the glass.
- Create a story within the frame by including a complementary object, such as a silver spoon, a recipe, an old cookie cutter, or a photo. And apply the KISS principle (Keep It Simple, Sweetie)—let the apron do the talking.

Decorate with your aprons by hanging a few from a dowel or curtain rod. Or secure a clothesline at each end of a window frame and pin upon it a selection of aprons. Or drape an apron on a padded hanger and hang it from a hook like a picture. Switch the aprons you have on display to give all of your aprons some air and appreciation.

every apron tells a story

Mary Winter

At about the time my kids were grown, I lost Taz, my faithful canine companion of fourteen years, and I was ready to make new memories with a new puppy—and a new dining room table. I wanted a table that reminded me of my grandmother's table, to help me reconnect to my past. As soon as the deliverymen left my new table, I realized this table wasn't anything like my grand- mother's table. Hers was large and sturdy, always covered with a white plastic table- cloth, its entire purpose function over form.

As a farmer's wife, she prepared an enormous amount of food. I don't ever remem- ber her consulting a cookbook, but she did love to sit in a chair next to the radio, wearing her bib apron, listening raptly as the county extension agent recited recipes that she jotted down on a tiny spiral tablet with the stub of a pencil. She cheerfully tested her recipes on us at daily meals and birthday parties and Sunday dinners, whether an elegant pot roast or a lemony fluff salad. When Grandma died, we sat in our chairs at her dining room table and wept. When the table and other contents of her home were sold in an estate sale, I took a special item to remember her by—her white cotton bib apron.

Making Memories

Not all aprons are precious relics. Though no less treasured, some are just plain done in, and these are the best kind to turn in to something memorable and new. Undo the stitches and seams of an apron with a seam ripper and gently pull it apart. You can use scraps of this fabric to make an apron quilt, entirely of old aprons. Or use scraps of different aprons to make an all-new patchwork-style apron.

WEAR DISPOSABLE GLOVES *when rifling through a thrift store bin or yard sale boxes when you're hunting for aprons.*

MY DAUGHTER, Angela, was born in 1967, and her grandma, Bernice Tuttle, sewed all of her clothes. When Angela was five, Bernice made an apron for Angela using scraps of material from every outfit she had ever sewn for her granddaughter. Thirty-eight years later, Angela's own daughter, Erin, wears this apron when she helps me bake cookies.

—Paula Tuttle

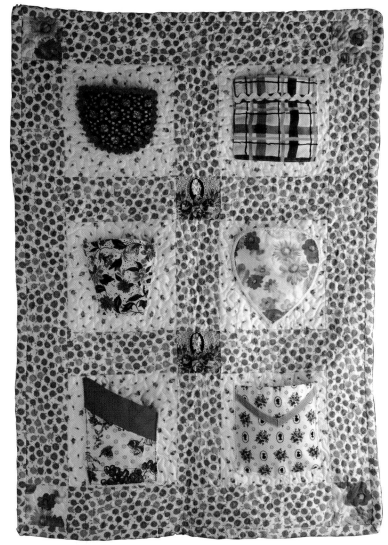

This sampler is decorated with repurposed apron pockets. Hung in a kitchen, the pockets could hold garlic or spices. By the telephone, it's the handy pencil, pad, keys, and sunglasses holder. In the bathroom or bedroom, it begs to be filled with potpourri, photos, or love letters.

Look for ways to make aprons into gifts that reflect the memories or sentiments of the recipient: a brightly colored waist or bib apron decorated with the pockets of a teenager's beloved (but retired) blue jeans; a custom-decorated chef's barbecue apron with treats pinned to the front—recipes or a gift certificate to a gourmet shop—and a packet of spicy rub in the pocket. One of my favorite memory aprons is the handprint apron. It's easy to make and as unique and special as, well, a handprint!

The Handprint Apron

WHEN MY three daughters were young, we created handprint aprons as a gift for each grandmother and one that I kept for myself. It's a real keepsake, and I only wear it on very special occasions.

—Kate Kelly

RECYCLE COTTON APRONS too raggedy to warrant saving into craft scraps for children's projects. And, of course, they make the best rags!

YOU WILL NEED: a purchased crisp, white chef's apron, a selection of fabric paints and pens, Styrofoam plates for the paint, paintbrushes, and newspaper.

Wash, dry, and iron the apron to preshrink. Practice making handprints on scrap paper first, to get a sense for how much paint you need and how to press your hand. Spread newspaper over a flat surface. Place the apron on the paper, front side up. Apply paint evenly to the palm and bottoms of your fingers—not too much paint or it will be goopy and drip. Spread out your fingers and press the palm and fingers onto the cloth, holding your hand firm and completely still for a slow count of five. Remove your hand carefully to avoid smudging. When the print is dry, write the handprinter's name and age next to it with a fabric pen. Heat set the prints according to the directions on the fabric paint package.

Have all the grandkids make a handprint on an apron for Grandma's birthday—or a whole classroom for a kindergarten teacher. Or make it a real heirloom by adding the handprint of a single child every year, say on the child's birthday.

every apron tells a story
Cheye Pagel

I love visiting my grandmother because we spend days together just talking and baking and sewing. One of my favorite summer memories involves Grandmother and me talking for hours and hours while we sewed clothes for my dolls. I sat at her feet and pushed the treadle on her old sewing machine, which she had taught me to use.

Grandmother always listens to me and pays attention to every word I say, no matter how much I go on. She also doesn't mind if I mess up on anything, especially when she's teaching me how to do something the right way. She is very patient—I hope that I will become as patient as she is.

Grandmother has sewn lots of aprons for me. My favorite one is a little half apron that is red and spotted with white hearts. It is put away because I do not want it to ever be harmed.

GRACE

AS PART of my ongoing use of words and text as inspiration for my visual arts projects, I chose to work with the word GRACE. It took me several years to identify a form that would convey the many meanings the word implies. Where was the one object, I asked myself, that would suggest movement, a prayer, a name, a state of being?

When I was given a 1950s-style chiffon hostess apron, purchased from a church bazaar sale as a gag gift, I knew I had found what I'd been looking for.

What could be more fitting for a GRACE project than an object with long, graceful ribbonlike ties, with a connection to meals over which grace is said, which may even have been worn by a gracious Southern lady named Grace? What actually clinched the use of the apron as my form, though, was the fact that this prototype, this apron I'd been given, had been lightly scorched when it had been ironed . . . its perfection was slightly flawed . . . it was itself a candidate for GRACE, that state of unconditional love and forgiveness.

—Judith Olson Gregory, artist

CREDITS

Photo Credits

STEVE BIGLEY: title page, ix, x, 2, 8, 13, 16, 17, 26, 28, 29, 30, 31, 39, 48, 50, 52, 57, 58, 60, 66, 67, 73, 76, 84, 91, 97 (top), 101, 102, 103, 104, 105, 106, 108, 109, 112, 113, 114, 115, 116, 119, 122, 123, 124, 125, 128, 129

CARMEN CAIRNS: 71, 75, 132

ELLYNANNE GEISEL: 53

CATHERINE HOPKINSON: 72, 79, 89, 93, 95

ELLEN JASKOL: 117, 127

CARL PETERSEN: 97

NANCY RICA SCHIFF: 98, 130, 131

MATTHEW SHAPERO: 70

JOHN WARK: 7, 59, 78, 81, 86, 107

p. 54: photo courtesy of Vonetta Lee

p. 56: photo courtesy of Betty Geer Johnson

p. 88: photo courtesy of Gina Marie Hayworth

p. 94: photo courtesy of Harold Sasaki

p. 99: photo courtesy of Hank Geisel

p. 110: photo courtesy of Jean Kornblueh Patiky

Other Credits

All pattern and apron illustrations by Mia Gonzales, Mia and Company Apparel Design, Pueblo, Colorado
miaandcompany@hotmail.com

p. 71: cupboard courtesy of Lena Velmere, Aladdin's Fine Treasures and Antique Mall, Pueblo, Colorado

p. 75: iron courtesy of Ronnie Crawford, All American Vogue, Denver, Colorado

p. 92: illustration from *the way to a man's heart*, page 18, Your Gas Range Cook Book, Your Home Service Department, THE GAS SERVICE COMPANY

p. 93: soda jerk accessories courtesy of Ronnie Crawford, All American Vogue, Denver Colorado; and Pueblo Refrigeration Equipment, Pueblo, Colorado

p. 110: Chicken Olivia Casserole recipe courtesy of Jane Levy, with permission by Nikki Dale-Oaster, Proprietor, HOGAN'S GROOVY GOURMET, Greensboro, North Carolina hogansgourmet@triad.rr.com

ACKNOWLEDGMENTS

❀

THIS BOOK is the joyful result of six years spent confirming my suspicion that I wasn't the only one who felt a connection to aprons. This odyssey unexpectedly brought into my life a bounty of friendship, trust, and the dearest people, to whom I owe special gratitude. I am forever appreciative to Karen Watts, my dream-come-true agent at Lark Productions, and my visionary editor at Andrews McMeel, Kelly Gilbert. Thank you also to:

Fran Weaver, Santa Barbara Writer's Conference founders Mary and Barnaby Conrad, and Marlo Faulkner, for their early and earnest encouragement; Judy Foreman, Susan Keller, and Rise Delmar Ochsner, my Santa Barbara cheerleaders and prime-time friends; Erin Owens and Carol Lombardo, for their unwavering belief in this project; Rose Jonas and Carol Weisman, for their humor and brilliance; Jack Canfield, for inspiring me that "going for it" was the only way to go; Jean Rather, for embracing this project and her generosity of heart.

Ellen Levine, to whom I owe particular thanks for inviting me to present my apron project to her and her staff at *Good Housekeeping* and for the subsequent article about me and my work. Thank you, thank you, thank you for writing the foreword to this book and for your genuine warmth and encouragement.

Liz Redecker, a talented seamstress with a heart of gold; Raelene Wilson, my dependable, creative graphic artist; Mary Ann Miklich, framing specialist; oral history enthusiast Dena Stevens and her sister, quilt artisan Paula Johnson; gracious hostess, Jane Levy: Hazel Manheimer, for opening her heart and guestroom; Ginny Ray Legare, girlhood best friend; and Kate Kelly, for reading an article about me and my aprons in her hometown newspaper and taking the time to write a letter of prophesy and support.

Photographers Nancy Rica Schiff, Ellen Jaskol, Steve Bigley, Carmen Cairns, Catherine Hopkinson, Carl Petersen, and Matthew Shapero, for capturing the spirit of the aprons and the spirited images of those wearing them.

My sons, Noah and Gideon, who are living their dreams and their happiness for me as I live mine. And to my husband, Hank, for his steadfast conviction that one day I'd be writing these grateful acknowledgments for an apron book!